A WORD IN SEASON

A WORD IN SEASON

AN ANTHOLOGY OF READINGS FROM THE FATHERS
FOR GENERAL USE

Editor
HENRY ASHWORTH, O.S.B.

Assistant Editors
ANNE FIELD, O.S.B.
EDITH BARNECUT, O.S.B.
MARY BERRY, C.S.A., M.A., PH.D. (CANTAB)
ROSEMARY MCCABE, M.A. (CANTAB)

VOLUME II
LENT: PART I

DUBLIN 1974
THE TALBOT PRESS

THE TALBOT PRESS LIMITED
P.O. Box 43A
Ballymount Road
Walkinstown, Dublin 12, Ireland
ISBN 0/85452/108/9
First published 1974

In this collection of readings from the Fathers the patristic texts of the Liturgy of the Hours have been used, together with additional material, to cover the two-year scheme of Scripture readings proposed as an optional alternative in the Roman Office. Passages selected for use with the three-year cycle of Sunday Gospels in the Mass Lectionary are also included. Translations have been made from the original languages.

ACKNOWLEDGEMENTS

No. 14 : *Lumen Gentium* : Geoffrey Chapman, 1966.
Nos. 25, 31, 41 : *Gaudium et Spes* : Catholic Truth Society translation.

Designed by Liam Miller
Set in Pilgrim type and printed in the Republic of Ireland
at the Dolmen Press, Dublin

CONTENTS

CONTENTS

CONTENTS

LENT

ASH WEDNESDAY

A reading from the Letter of Pope St Clement I to the Corinthians.

Cap. 7, 4-8, 3; 8, 5-9, 1; 13, 1-4; 19, 2 : SC 167, 111, 113, 115, 121, 133.

Repent

Let us fix our gaze on the blood of Christ, and learn how precious it is to God, his Father. Poured out for our salvation, it has won the grace of repentance for the whole human race. We have only to recall past generations to see that the Lord has always offered the opportunity of repentance to those willing to return to him. This was the burden of Noah's preaching, and all who listened to him were saved. Jonah proclaimed destruction to the Ninevites: they repented and their pleas for mercy placated God's anger and saved them, even though they were not of his chosen people.

The ministers of God's grace have all been inspired by the Holy Spirit to speak of repentance. The Lord of the universe himself has spoken of it with an oath. *As I live, says the Lord, it is not a sinner's death that I desire, but his conversion;* and he adds the gracious assurance : *House of Israel, repent of your wickedness. Say to the children of my people : Even if your sins reach from earth to heaven, even if they are redder than scarlet, blacker than sackcloth, you have only to turn to me with your whole heart and say 'Father!' and I will listen to you, as to a holy people.*

By his own almighty will, therefore, he has ratified his desire to give all his loved ones the chance to return to him. Let us bow then to that sublime and glorious will, throw ourselves on his mercy, and humbly beseech his goodness and compassion. No more energy must be wasted in the wrangling and jealousy that can only lead to death.

Let us be humble, brothers, and obeying the Scriptures, have done with all arrogance and senseless anger. As the Holy Spirit says, *The wise man must not boast of his wisdom, the strong of his strength, the rich of his wealth. No; anyone who boasts should make his boast in the Lord, seeking the Lord, and acting with justice and integrity.* He should especially remember the words of the Lord Jesus that teach gentleness and forbearance, for he said : *Be merciful, that you may have mercy shown you; forgive, that you may be forgiven. As you treat others, so you will be treated; as you give, so you will receive; as you judge, so you will be judged. If you are kind to others, you also will be dealt with kindly. The measure of your giving will be the measure of your receiving.*

Let this rule, these commands, strengthen our resolve to live in lowly obedience to his sacred words, for *to whom shall I show favour,* says Holy Scripture, *but to him who is gentle and peaceable and trembles at my words?*

Inspired by the many great and glorious examples of the past, we are called upon now to return quickly to the peace we have always been taught to pursue, and, with our eyes on the Father and Creator of the whole world, to cling firmly to this, his sublime and all-surpassing gift.

YEAR II

A reading from a Sermon of Pope St Leo the Great.
Tract 48, 1. CCL 138A 279-280.

*The whole body of the Church must be cleansed
from all defilement*

Of all the days celebrated in varying degrees of solemnity by the Christian liturgy, beloved brethren, none ranks higher than

the paschal feast, by which the whole series of festivals is consecrated and confirmed in honour in the Church of God. If it is
true that the very birth of our Lord from his mother looked
forward to its culmination in this mystery, then it is clear that
the sole purpose of God's Son in being born was to make his
crucifixion possible. For in the Virgin's womb he assumed mortal
flesh, and in this mortal flesh the unfolding of his passion was
accomplished. Thus the mercy of God fulfilled a plan too deep
for words: Christ's humanity became for us a redemptive
sacrifice, annulment of sin, and the first-fruits of resurrection to
eternal life.

When we consider what the entire world owes to our Lord's
cross, we realize our need to prepare for the celebration of
Easter by a fast of forty days if we are to take part worthily in
these sacred mysteries. Not only ought every defilement to be
purged away from bishops who have received the fullness of the
Sacrament of Order, from priests who hold the second place,
and from deacons who administer the sacraments, but the whole
body of the Church and entire company of the faithful must be
purified, so that in the temple of God, whose foundation is its
founder himself, every stone may be beautiful and every section
radiant. If it is reasonable to embellish a king's palace or governor's residence with every ornamental art, so that the greater a
man's importance the more splendid his dwelling, what zeal
ought to be expended in building the house of God himself, and
how distinguished should be its furnishing! No doubt such a
task can be neither undertaken nor completed without the
architect; nevertheless the builder of the house has given it the
power to grow in stature through its own efforts. For in the
erection of this temple living and intelligent materials are being
used, which of their own free will assemble themselves into a
single structure at the prompting of the Spirit of grace. There
was a time when they neither loved God nor sought him; but he

loved and sought them so that they might begin to love and seek him in return. This is what the blessed apostle John speaks of when he says: *Let us love God, for he first loved us.*

Since therefore the entire company of the faithful and each believer in particular form one and the same temple of God, there must be the same perfection in each individual as there is in the whole; for even if all are not alike in beauty nor is there equal merit in such a diversity of membership, yet the bond of love ensures communion of beauty between them all. While those who are united in holy love may not all have received the same gifts of grace, they rejoice nonetheless in their mutual blessings. Nothing that they love can be wanting to them, for by finding happiness in the progress of others they increase their own store of riches.

THURSDAY AFTER ASH WEDNESDAY

YEAR I

A reading from the Sermons of St Leo the Great.
6th Sermon for Lent, 1-2. PL 54, 285-287.

Spiritual purification through fasting and works of mercy

The earth, dearest brethren, is indeed always filled with the mercy of the Lord, and nature itself teaches every one of the faithful to worship God, since heaven and earth, the sea and all they contain proclaim the goodness and might of their creator, and the marvellous beauty of the elements that are placed at man's service calls for corresponding gratitude on the part of him who represents all creatures endowed with reason.

And now as once again we draw near to those days immediately preceding the paschal feast which more specifically recall the mystery of man's redemption, a more earnest purification of our hearts is asked of us. The paschal solemnity is especially characterised by the joy of the entire Church in the forgiveness of sins; not only of those newly born in baptism, but also of those long since numbered among the adopted sons of God. For although men are made new chiefly through the waters of baptismal regeneration, an additional daily renewal is granted us to counteract the wear and tear of our perishable nature. No matter what degree of perfection a man has attained, there is no one who ought not to be always advancing in goodness, and therefore it must be our common endeavour that the Day of Redemption may find no one among us who has grown old in sin.

At this season, therefore, dearest brethren, we must carry out with even greater care and commitment what Christians should regard as their duty at all times, observing the apostolic institution of Lent by abstaining not only from food, but above all from sin. Nothing, however, is more profitably associated with spiritual exercises and holy fasting than almsgiving. This includes many praiseworthy actions under the heading of works of mercy, and makes it possible for all the faithful to be equal in goodwill, even though their resources may not be the same. Nothing, in fact, can ever so obstruct the love we owe to both God and man as to prevent our will being always free to choose to do good. Indeed, according to those words of the angels, *Glory to God in the highest, and on earth peace to men of good will*, anyone who shows loving compassion towards those in distress will be blessed not only with the virtue of goodwill but also with the gift of peace.

The works of mercy are extremely comprehensive, and their very variety means that all true Christians, the poor and the moderately endowed as well as the rich, can take their share in the giving of alms; even if the means at their disposal are disparate, they may yet be equal in readiness of heart.

A reading from the Sermons of St John Chrysostom.
Oratio 3 adversus Judaeos : PG 48, 867-868.

*We fast because of our sins, while we are preparing
to approach the sacred mysteries*

Why do we fast for forty days? Formerly many believers
approached the sacraments without any particular preparation,
especially at the time when Christ first gave them to us. But
when the Fathers realized the harm that could result from such
neglect, they took counsel together and decreed that a period of
forty days of fasting be set aside, during which the people would
meet to pray and listen to the word of God. During this Lenten
season each of the faithful would undergo a thorough purification by means of prayer, almsgiving, fasting, watching,
repentant tears, confession, and every other remedial measure.
Then when they had done all in their power to cleanse their
consciences, they could approach the sacraments.

It is certain that the Fathers did well to use such lenience in
their desire to establish us in the habit of fasting. For, as we
know, we could proclaim a fast throughout the whole year, and
no one would pay any attention. But now, with a set time for
fasting of only forty days, even the most sluggish needs no
exhortation to rouse himself to undergo it; he accepts it as a
regular observance and recurring encouragement.

So, when someone asks you why you fast, you should not
answer : because of the Passover, or because of the cross. Neither
of these is the reason for our fasting. We fast because of our
sins, since we are preparing to approach the sacred mysteries.
Moreover, the Christian Passover is a time for neither fasting
nor mourning, but for great joy. For the cross destroyed sin and
made expiation for the whole world. It reconciled ancient

enmities, and opened the gates of heaven. It made friends of those who had been filled with hatred, restoring them to the citizenship of heaven. Through the cross our human nature has been set at the right hand of the throne of God, and we have been granted countless good things besides. Therefore we must not give way to mourning or sadness, but rejoice greatly instead over all these blessings.

Listen to the exultant words of St Paul: *God forbid that I should boast of anything but the cross of our Lord Jesus Christ.* And elsewhere he writes: *God shows his own love for us, because when we were still sinners Christ died for our sake.*

St John's message is the same. *God loved the world so much,* he declares, and then passing over every other manifestation of God's love, he comes at once to the crucifixion. *God loved the world so much that he gave his only Son,* that is, he gave him up to be crucified, *so that all who believed in him might not perish but might have eternal life.* If, then, the cross has its foundation in love and is our glory, we must not say we mourn because of the cross. Far from it. What we have to mourn over is our own sins, and that is why we fast.

FRIDAY AFTER ASH WEDNESDAY

YEAR I

A reading from the Homilies of St John Chrysostom.
Hom. de diabolo tentatore 2, 6 : PG 49, 263-264.

The five ways of repentance

There are many different ways of repentance, all of which lead to heaven. Let us consider them.

The first is condemnation of our own sins. *Begin by confessing your sins if you wish to be justified.* In the words of the prophet, *I said, I will confess my sins to the Lord, and you, Lord, have forgiven the wickedness of my heart.* If we condemn our own sins, therefore, we already have a sufficient claim to forgiveness. By doing so, we shall less easily fall into them again. We must make our own conscience our accuser, if we wish to avoid being accused before the Lord's tribunal.

This first way of repentance is an excellent one, but there is a second, in no way inferior to it: not to bear malice against our enemies, to overcome anger, to forgive the sins of our fellow-servants; then we shall be forgiven our offences against the Lord. This, then, is the second way of making amends for our sins. If we forgive men their sins, our heavenly Father will also forgive ours.

Let us now learn the third way of repentance. It is to pray fervently and attentively from our inmost heart.

Giving to the poor is the fourth way, and it is exceedingly powerful.

If we live a life of simplicity and humility, it will wear down our inclination to sin just as effectively as any of the four previous ways. Remember that tax collector who had nothing to offer but his humility, and this was enough to free him of his heavy burden of guilt.

We have now described five ways of repentance: first, condemnation of our sins; second, forgiving the offences of others; third, prayer; fourth, giving to the poor; fifth, humility. There is therefore no room for idleness; we must follow these ways day after day. They are easy enough; poverty is no excuse. Even if we live a life of the utmost poverty, we shall still be able to restrain our anger, to be humble, to pray unceasingly and to condemn our own sins, and in no way does our empty purse cause any difficulty. Not even when we follow the way that involves giving to the poor — not even there is poverty any obstacle to carrying out the command. Remember the widow who could only give two small coins.

Now that we have learnt the remedies for our ills, let us always put them to good use. When we are fully restored to spiritual health, we shall then be ready to take part in the heavenly banquet with complete confidence. In great happiness we shall come face to face with the King of glory and gain everlasting blessings, by the grace and merciful love of our Lord Jesus Christ.

YEAR II

A reading from the Homilies of St John Chrysostom.
Supp. Hom. 6 De precatione : PG 64, 462-466.

Prayer is the light of the soul

Prayer and communion with God constitute the highest good, for they bring us into fellowship and union with him. Just as contact with earthly light enables our eyes to see, so when we gaze on God our heart is flooded with his light which is beyond all description. The prayer I speak of is not a mechanical formula, but a movement of the heart; it is not confined to fixed times and seasons, but continues night and day. It is not only at set hours of prayer that we should turn our minds to God; we need to do it also at those times when we are busy with our occupations, helping the poor or engaged in any of the other works of mercy, so that remembrance of God and desire for him permeate all that we do. Then our actions, as though seasoned with the love of God, will become a pleasing offering to the Lord of all, and we ourselves, by thus filling every moment with prayer, shall enjoy great spiritual profit throughout our lives.

Prayer is the light of the soul, by which we acquire true knowledge of God. It is the medium of communication between God and man. Through prayer our hearts are raised to heaven and we embrace God in a way no words can convey. Like an infant crying for its mother, so do our souls crave the divine nourishment. We ask for our own needs, and we receive gifts surpassing the whole visible creation.

Prayer is a worthy ambassador before God, which makes the heart joyful and gives peace to the soul. And when I speak of prayer, you are not to imagine I mean words. Prayer is the desire for God, a wordless love, an attitude of sonship not of man's originating but actuated by divine grace. *We do not know how we ought to pray*, declares St Paul, *but in our inarticulate groans it is the Spirit himself who is interceding for us.* For anyone to whom the Lord has granted this kind of prayer, it is a treasure which can never be lost, a heavenly food to satisfy our souls. Once we have tasted it, an eternal longing for the Lord burns in our hearts with a fierce intensity.

Therefore, in preparing to receive him, with lowly hearts we shall paint the walls of our homes and illuminate them with the light of righteousness. With the gold leaf of good works we shall adorn them and enrich them with the mosaics of enduring faith. Then over all, in completion, we shall place the roof of prayer, to make our homes perfect for the Lord. So we shall receive him as in a splendid palace. And by his grace we shall henceforth keep him like an image set up in the temple of our souls.

SATURDAY AFTER ASH WEDNESDAY

A reading from the Apostolic Constitution *Poenitemini* of Pope Paul VI.
AAS t. 58 (1966) 178-179.

Be converted to the living God

The religious significance of penance is revealed in the Old Testament with ever-increasing clarity. Men may have done penance after sin in order to appease the divine anger, or when they were stricken by serious calamities or threatened by personal dangers, or when they were trying to obtain God's favours; but their outward practice of penance was always united with an interior attitude of conversion, by which they turned away from sin with their whole hearts and returned to God with renewed fervour. Indeed, even after their sins had been forgiven, and even when they were not seeking to obtain any particular benefit from the Lord, men fasted and stripped themselves of their possessions, offering prayer and worship to God and adding almsgiving to their privations. They abstained from food and wore sackcloth in order to afflict themselves, to humble themselves before God, to seek his face, to dispose themselves to prayer, to understand the things of God more clearly, to prepare themselves to meet their God. Already, then, in the Old Testament penance appears as a religious and personal act, the ultimate purpose of which is to make us begin to love God and surrender ourselves to him. Fasting must be for God's sake, not our own.

Such also was the character penance was meant to possess in those practices which were prescribed and regulated by the Law. When they failed to produce this effect, the Lord complained: *The fasting you have done up till now will never make your voice heard on high. It is your hearts, not your garments, that must be torn.*

Nor is penance in the Old Testament without what may be called its social aspect. The penitential rites of the ancient covenant not only brought a collective realization of sin, but were conditional to membership of the People of God. We may notice also that even before the birth of Christ, penance is presented as a means and sign of perfection and holiness. Judith, Daniel, the prophetess Anna, and many other noble souls served God joyfully and gladly day and night in fasting and prayer.

Finally, among the just of the Old Testament there were some whose personal penance atoned for the sins of the whole community; for example Moses, who fasted for forty days in order to appease the Lord's anger over the sins of his faithless people. Here, above all, appears the figure of the Servant of the Lord, who bore our infirmities and upon whom the Lord laid the guilt of us all.

But all these were only shadows of the things to come. Penance is attested as an essential element in the spiritual life by the religious experience of mankind and is the object of a special precept of divine revelation; but it assumes a new and incomparably deeper significance in Christ and in his Church.

YEAR II

A reading from the fourth book of St Irenaeus 'Against Heresies'. 13, 4-14, 1 : SC 100, 534-540.

Friendship with God

In the beginning, God created Adam because he wished for someone upon whom he could bestow his benefits. For his own part, he had no need of man, for before Adam, before anything was created, the Word gave glory to his Father, dwelt in him, and was himself glorified by the Father, as we know from his own words: *Father, glorify me with the glory that I had with you before the world was made.*

Nor was it because he needed our service that he commanded us to follow him, but simply in order to save us. For to follow the Saviour is to share in his salvation, even as to follow the light is to share in the light. Those who live in the light do not cause it to shine, but are themselves illumined and made radiant by the light. They contribute nothing to the light, but receive the whole benefit themselves by being illumined by the light.

So is it also with our service of God. God gains no advantage from it; he has no need of our obedience. Nevertheless, upon those who follow him and serve him, he confers life, incorruptibility and eternal glory. He rewards those who serve him for their service, and those who follow him for their obedience, but derives no benefit from them, for he is rich and perfect, in need of nothing.

But he is also good and merciful, and this is why he seeks the service of men; for if they persevere in his service he intends, as their reward, to admit them into communion with himself, knowing as he does that their need of this is equalled only by his own freedom from any need.

For this is man's glory: to persevere in God's service. Our Lord's words to his disciples, *You did not choose me; it is I who chose you,* were meant to teach them this. They were doing him no honour by following him, but because they followed him they were themselves honoured by the Son of God. On another occasion our Lord declared: *It is my wish that where I am, they also may be with me, so that they may see my glory.* He did not say this out of vanity, but because of his desire to share his own glory with his disciples.

A reading from the Letter of Pope St Clement I to the Corinthians.
Cap. 49-50. SC 167, 181-183.

> *How strong a bond the love of God creates !*
> *Who can express its power?*

Anyone truly possessed by the love of Christ is bound to keep his commandments. How strong a bond the love of God creates! Who can express its power, or find words for the radiance of its beauty? Beyond all description are the heights to which it raises us. Love unites us to God; it *cancels innumerable sins*, it has no limit to its endurance, it bears everything patiently. Love is neither servile nor arrogant. It does not provoke schisms or form factions, but always acts in harmony with others. By it all God's chosen ones have been sanctified; without it, it is impossible to please him. Out of love the Lord took us to himself; because he loved us and it was God's will, our Lord Jesus Christ gave his life's-blood for us — he gave his flesh for our flesh, his life for our lives.

See then, beloved, what a great and wonderful thing love is, and how inexpressible its perfection. Who are worthy to possess it unless God makes them so? To him, therefore, we must turn, begging of his mercy that there may be found in us a love free from human partiality and beyond reproach. Every generation has passed away from Adam's time until our own, but those who, by God's grace, were made perfect in love have a dwelling now among the saints, and when at last the kingdom of Christ appears, they will be revealed. *Take shelter in your rooms for a little while*, says Scripture, *until my wrath subsides. Then I will remember a day of gladness, and I will raise you from your graves.*

Beloved, it is by keeping God's commandments, and living together in harmony that we shall find happiness, for the love we show to one another will win us the forgiveness of our sins. As Scripture says: *Happy are those whose transgressions are pardoned, whose sins are forgiven. Happy the man to whom the Lord imputes no fault, on whose lips there is no guile.* This is the blessing given those whom God has chosen through Jesus Christ our Lord. To him be glory for ever and ever.   Amen.

YEAR II

A reading from the Letters of St Augustine.
Epist 140, 13-15, seu De Gratia N.T. Liber; PL 33, 2 : col. 543-544.

Christ gives those who love him a share in his sufferings

When the time came for the grace of the New Testament to be revealed through the man Christ Jesus, there was no question of his attracting us to himself with the promise of earthly happiness. This explains our Lord's willingness to undergo suffering, to be scourged, spat upon, mocked, nailed to the cross, and to accept death itself like one conquered and humiliated. All this he endured so that those who believed in him might learn what recompense for their dutiful service they could ask for and expect from the God who made them his sons. They had to learn to serve him without any eye to earthly prosperity, for to value their faith at so low a price would be tantamount to rejecting it and trampling it underfoot.

By his great human compassion and by appearing among us in the form of a servant, Christ, who is both God and man, meant to teach us what we should spurn in this life and what we should hope for in the next. It was accordingly at the very height of his passion, when his enemies thought they had won such a mighty victory, that he gave voice to our human weakness which was being crucified together with our former selves to set our sinful bodies free; and his cry was *My God, my God, why have you forsaken me?*

In taking up this expression of our frailty our Head is praying the psalm: *My God, my God, look upon me; why have you forsaken me?* Here the suppliant feels abandoned; his prayer seems to be of no avail. Jesus made these words his own; they are the words of his Body, that is, of the Church which must endure the travail of conversion from unregenerate human nature into the new creation. His is the voice of our human weakness, which has to be weaned from the good things of the Old Testament and taught to long after and hope for those of the New.

YEAR A. Mt 4: 1-10

A reading from the Homilies of St Gregory Nazianzen.
Oratio 40. 10 : PG 36, 370-371.

Christians have the means of conquering temptation

We must not expect baptism to free us from the temptations of our persecutor. The body that concealed him made even the Word of God a target for the enemy; his assumption of a visible form made even the invisible light an object of attack. Nevertheless, since we have at hand the means of overcoming our enemy, we must have no fear of the struggle. Flaunt in his face the water and the Spirit. In them will be extinguished all the flaming darts of the evil one.

Suppose the tempter makes us feel the pinch of poverty, as he did even to Christ, and, taking advantage of our hunger, talks of turning stones into bread; we must not be taken in by him, but let him learn what he has still not grasped. Refute him with the word of life, with the word that is the bread sent down from heaven and that gives life to the world.

He may try to ensnare us through our vanity, as he tried to ensnare Christ when he set him on the pinnacle of the temple and said: 'Prove your divinity — throw yourself down.' Let us beware of succumbing to pride, for the tempter will by no means stop at one success. He is never satisfied, and is always pursuing us. Often he beguiles us with something good and useful, but its end is always evil. That is simply his method of waging war.

We also know how well-versed the devil is in Scripture. When Christ answered the temptation to turn stones into bread with a rebuke from Scripture beginning: *It is written*, the devil countered with the same words, tempting Christ to throw himself down from the pinnacle of the temple. *For it is written*, he quoted, *he will give his angels charge of you, and on their hands they will bear you up.* O past master of all evil, why suppress the verse that follows? You did not finish the quotation, but I know full well what it means: that we shall tread on you as on an adder and a basilisk; protected by the Trinity, we shall trample on you as on serpents and on scorpions.

If the tempter tries to overthrow us through our greed, showing us at one glance all the kingdoms of the world — as if they belonged to him — and demanding that we fall down and worship him, we should despise him, for we know him to be a penniless impostor. Strong in our baptism, each of us can say: 'I too am made in the image of God, but, unlike you, I have not yet become an outcast from heaven through my pride. I have put on Christ; by my baptism I have become one with him. It is you that should fall prostrate before me.' At these words he can only surrender and retire in shame; as he retreated before Christ, the light of the world, so will he depart from those illumined by that light. Such are the gifts conferred by baptism on those who understand its power; such the rich banquet it lays before those who hunger for the things of the spirit.

YEAR B. Mk 1 : 12-15

A reading from St Augustine's Commentary on the Psalms.
Ps. 60, 2-3; CCL 39, 766.

> *In Christ we were put to the test, and in him we have overcome the devil*

Hear my cry, O God; listen to my prayer. Whose words are these? One might think they were spoken by some individual person. But can this really be so, when he goes on to say : *From the ends of the earth I call to you, with a heart in torment.* These are evidently not the words of a man speaking for himself alone. And yet, after all, the speaker *is* a single person, for it is the one Christ who calls out, the Christ of whom we are all members. It is his heritage that calls from the ends of the earth, those heirs of his of whom the Son was told : *Ask, and I will give you the nations for your heritage, the ends of the earth for your domain.*

So it is what belongs to Christ, Christ's heritage, Christ's body, Christ's one Church; it is this oneness, which we are, that calls from the ends of the earth. And what does it call out? What I said just now : *Hear my cry, O God, listen to my prayer. From the ends of the earth I call to you.* This is my cry to you from the ends of the earth, that is to say from everywhere.

But why do I cry to you in this way? *Because my heart is in torment.* Throughout the whole world, in every race under the sun, Christ manifests that he is present, not in immense glory, but in severe trial and testing. Life for us, as we journey on,

171

must indeed have its testing times, for by their means we make progress, learning our true worth by being put to the test. There can be no crown without victory, no victory without contest, no contest without adversary and testing.

So it is the whole Christ in torment who cries from the ends of the earth, but he is not left forsaken; for it was his will to include all of us who are his body in that body of his in which he has already died, risen again, and ascended into heaven. This was to assure his members that we too shall follow where our Head has gone before us. That is why the Lord Jesus Christ summed us all up in his own person when he allowed Satan to put him to the test. We have just read in the gospel that the devil tempted him in the wilderness. But it was the whole Christ that was put to the test, for in Christ you also were tempted, since he took to himself human nature from you, and salvation came to you from him. From you he incurred death, but from him you gained life. From you insults were his lot, but from him honours were your award. In your flesh, then, he allowed himself to be tested, and in him you were victorious.

If in Christ we are put to the test, in him we overcome the devil. Can one think of Christ being put to the test, and not go on to think of how he gained the mastery? See yourself being put to the test in him, then see yourself gaining the mastery with him. He could have forbidden the devil to assail him; but if he had not allowed himself to be tempted, he could not have shown you how to conquer in your own time of trial.

A reading from the Homilies on the Song of Songs by Origen.
Hom. III : GCS, t. 8, 221, 19-223, 5.

*Jesus was tempted by the devil to teach the Church that the way
to him was through many tribulations and trials*

At every turning in our mortal life we are in danger of being
ensnared by sin, caught in the nets concealed in our path by that
mighty hunter opposed to the Lord named Nimrod, who is in
fact none other than the devil, the adversary of God himself.
These cleverly laid snares of temptation are called, therefore,
the toils of the devil.

There came a time when the enemy had spread his nets in all
directions, and almost all the world was entangled in them. And
so it was that someone had to come who was strong and mighty
enough to destroy them, so as to open up the way for those who
would follow him. Such was our Saviour. Before he entered into
union and fellowship with the Church, he suffered the temptation of the devil, so that he might call the Church to him
across a path cleared of the tempter's nets. Thus, undoubtedly,
he means to teach us, by his own example, that the way to Christ
for us is not along the primrose path of ease but through many
tribulations and trials.

No other was there but Christ himself who could have overcome the toils of the devil, for as Scripture says, *All have sinned;*
and elsewhere, *There is not a righteous man on earth who does
good and never sins.* There is also the text : *No one is free from
stain, not even the day-old infant.* Only Jesus, our Lord and
Saviour, committed no sin, but for our sake the Father made him
into sin, so that offered for sin in the likeness of sinful flesh, he
might condemn sin. And so our Saviour was led into temptation

as we are, but only he was able to avoid being entangled in the devil's toils; indeed, his bursting them asunder and destroying them gave his Church the courage henceforth to trample down the snares and pass by the nets, saying with gladness: *Our soul has escaped like a bird from the fowler's snare; the snare is broken, and we have escaped.* None was able to break the snare but only he whom it could not hold.

Our Saviour did indeed submit to death, but it was of his own free will, and not, as with us, from necessity, on account of sin. In death he alone was free from death's power, and so able to vanquish the one that wielded it, and deliver all who were held in its thrall. Thus at one and the same time he raised from the dead both himself and death's bondsmen, enthroning them with himself in heaven. *When he ascended on high he led a host of captives*, raising not only their souls, but their bodies as well. As we are told in St Matthew's gospel: *Many bodies of the saints were raised, and appeared to many; and they went into Jerusalem, the city of the living God.*

MONDAY

YEAR I

A reading from the Dogmatic Constitution on the Church.
Lumen Gentium 2, 16.

Behold, I shall save my people

By an utterly free and mysterious decree of his own wisdom and goodness, the eternal Father created the whole world. His plan was to dignify men with a participation in his own divine life. He did not abandon men after they had fallen in Adam, but ceaselessly offered them helps to salvation, in anticipation of Christ the Redeemer, who is *the image of the invisible God, the firstborn of every creature.* All the elect, before time began, the Father *foreknew and predestined to become conformed to the image of his Son, so that he should be the firstborn among many brethren.*

He planned to assemble in the holy Church all those who would believe in Christ. Already from the beginning of the world the foreshadowing of the Church took place. She was prepared for in a remarkable way throughout the history of the people of Israel and by means of the Old Covenant. Established in the present era of time, the Church was made manifest by the outpouring of the Spirit. At the end of time she will achieve her glorious fulfilment. Then, as may be read in the holy Fathers, all just men from the time of Adam, *from Abel, the just one, to the last of the elect,* will be gathered together with the Father in the universal Church.

Those who have not yet received the gospel are related in various ways to the People of God. In the first place there is the people to whom the covenants and the promises were given and from whom Christ was born according to the flesh. On account of their fathers, this people remains most dear to God, for God does not repent of the gifts he makes nor of the calls he issues.

But the plan of salvation also includes those who acknowledge the Creator. In the first place among these are the Moslems, who, professing to hold the faith of Abraham, along with us adore the one and merciful God, who on the last day will judge mankind. Nor is God himself far distant from those who in shadows and images seek the unknown God, for it is he who gives to all men life and breath and every other gift, and who as Saviour wills that all men be saved.

Those also can attain to everlasting salvation who through no fault of their own do not know the gospel of Christ or his Church, yet sincerely seek God and, moved by grace, strive by their deeds to do his will as it is known to them through the dictates of conscience. Nor does divine providence deny the help necessary for salvation to those who, without blame on their part, have not yet arrived at an explicit knowledge of God, but who strive to live a good life, thanks to his grace. Whatever goodness or truth is found among them is looked upon by the Church as a preparation for the gospel. She regards such qualities as given by him who enlightens all men so that they may finally have life.

YEAR II

A reading from a Sermon by St Gregory Nazianzen on the Love of the Poor.
Oratio 14, 23-25; PG 35, 888-889.

*Let us show kindness to our fellow-men as the Lord
has shown kindness to us*

Do we wonder how it is that we come to exist, to breathe, to think and understand, above all to know God, to hope for the kingdom of heaven and the full and perfect vision in the future of what we now see only dimly as if in a mirror? We know we are the sons of God, joint heirs with Christ, and (if I dare say it) even made divine ourselves; but to what and to whom do we owe all this? Or, to speak of the ordinary things we see around us, by whose free gift do we contemplate the sky's beauty, the sun's course, the moon's disk, the myriads of stars; and who has established the whole universe in order and harmony, like a well-tuned lyre? Who has given us rain, crops to cultivate, food and drink? What of our arts and crafts, the homes we live in, our laws and government, our civilization, our families and friends? And who has given us the animals we either train for our service or raise for our sustenance? In short, who has appointed us to be lords and masters of the earth, and made man the superior being that he is? Surely God, who now asks us to show kindness to all our fellow-men in return for his accumulated benefits. We have received so much from him and hope for still more; should we not be ashamed to refuse him this one request, this love for our brothers? He is our God and Master, yet he is not ashamed to be called our Father; shall we, then, refuse to acknowledge our own kith and kin? No, my friends and brothers, let us not be unjust stewards of all that God has given us, or we may hear Peter saying to us, *Shame on you, who withhold from others what is their due! Make God's impartial justice your model, and then there will be no poor among you.*

Do not let us wear ourselves out amassing and guarding wealth while others are toiling in poverty, or we may hear the stinging threats of Amos saying to us, *Listen to this, you who say 'When will the new moon be over, so that we can sell corn? And when will the sabbath be past, so that we can resume business?'* Let us rather model ourselves on the foremost and greatest commandment of God, who sends down rain on the just and the unjust, and makes his sun shine on all alike. At the creation, when the soil had not yet been tilled, he gave the freedom of the earth with its springs, rivers and woods to all the inhabitants of dry land. The air he gave to birds and the sea to water-creatures; upon all he bestowed life's basic needs in abundance. Nothing had to be acquired by force, restricted by law, or separated by boundaries. Though everything was given to be enjoyed by all in common, the copiousness of the supply was not thereby diminished. All creatures were equal in value and held in equal honour by God, who, in giving to all alike, displayed the riches of his own bountiful goodness.

TUESDAY

A reading from the Homilies of St John Chrysostom on the Letter to the Romans.
Hom. 14, 8 : PG 60, 534-535.

What is there that God has not done for us?

There is nothing that God has not done for us. He made the world corruptible on our account, and on our account again he made it incorruptible. For our sake he allowed his prophets to be ill-treated; for our sake he let them be taken into captivity, fall into the furnace and undergo countless other afflictions. Indeed it was for our sake that he called them to their prophetic task and summoned others to be apostles. For our sake the Son of God suffered opprobrium; in the words of Scripture, *Taunts against you have fallen on me*. And when we still rebel, even after receivings such great blessings, God does not abandon us, but calls us once more and raises up others to intercede for grace on our behalf. Moses was one of these; for it was only in order to move him to make entreaty for the people that God said to Moses : *Let me destroy these people altogether*.

Even now God acts in the same way. He grants the gift of prayer not because he needs our supplication, but to prevent our growing careless through receiving a salvation that costs us no effort. Therefore he declares he has often been reconciled with men for the sake of David or for the sake of this person or that; by such means he seeks to show the principle on which reconciliation with God is established. His love for men might have appeared greater if he had told them that his anger was appeased on his own account instead of for the sake of someone else; but this would not have furthered his purpose, since he did not want reconciliation with God to be a matter of indifference to those who were saved.

This is the explanation of his saying to Jeremiah : *Do not pray for these people, because I will not listen to you.* His intention was to put fear into the people, rather than to stop Jeremiah praying; the prophet understood, and continued to plead for them. Just as God pronounced his decree to the Ninevites without qualification or offer of hope, and thus led them through fear to repentance, so his purpose in this episode was to stir up the people and inspire greater respect for their prophet, in order to induce them at least by this means to pay attention. Then, as their frenzy proved incurable and they were not brought to their senses even by the deportation of their brethren, he first of all exhorted them to remain where they were. They refused to do so, and went of their own accord to Egypt. Even this he tolerated, but begged them not to involve themselves in impiety as well as deserting to Egypt. And when they disobeyed again, he sent the prophet with them to prevent their complete and final ruin.

Was there anything the prophets did not suffer on account of the people? They were sawn asunder, driven out, reproached, stoned; they bore innumerable other injuries, but each time they went back to the people again. Samuel, for instance, never ceased to mourn for Saul, despite the grievous insults and unbearable affronts he had received from him. He allowed none of these things to remain in his memory. Jeremiah composed and wrote down lamentations for the Jews, and although the Persian governor would have allowed him to live in security and complete freedom wherever he wished, he preferred to share the people's maltreatment and to endure the miseries of exile with them, rather than stay at home.

A reading from St Cyprian's Treatise on the Lord's Prayer.
Cap 1-3 : CSEL 3, 267-268.

He who gave us life has also taught us how to pray

My dear brethren, the gospel teachings are divine commands, foundations on which we may build our hope, a sure basis for our belief, nourishment for our hearts, signposts to guide us on our journey, and a means of help towards salvation. For by instructing the receptive minds of the faithful on earth, they lead them to the kingdom of heaven.

It was God's will that through his servants, the prophets, many things should be revealed; but far more important are the utterances of God's own Son, his Word. It was he, indeed, who had already spoken to us through the prophets, but now, in his own person, he addresses us directly. No longer are we to prepare the way for one who is to come; for now he comes himself, opening up the way and pointing it out to us. Until now we have been wandering, blind and helpless, in the darkness of death, but now in the full light of grace we are able to keep to the way of life under the guidance and leadership of the Lord himself.

Besides the other lifegiving precepts and divine commands with which Christ has sought to ensure salvation to his people, he has also given us his own form of prayer, so making clear to us what we ought to pray for. Thus he who gave us life has also taught us how to pray. The loving kindness that led him to give us all that we have has also prompted him to instruct us in prayer, so that when we speak to the Father in the very words that his Son has taught us, we may be more certain of being heard.

He had already foretold the hour when every sincere worshipper would pray to the Father in spirit and in truth, and now the time was ripe for the fulfilment of his promise that we, who were to draw from his own essential holiness our share of the spiritual and the true, should learn from his own lips how to offer to the Father true and spiritual worship.

For what prayer can be more truly spiritual than that given by Christ himself who sent the Holy Spirit down upon us? And what prayer can sound more true to the Father than that which issued from the mouth of the Son who himself is truth? To pray in any other way than he has taught us would be not merely ignorant but blameworthy; this he has himself made clear by saying: *You have rejected God's command for the sake of your own tradition.*

Let us then, my dear brethren, pray as God our Master has taught us. Such a prayer will strike upon the Father's ear with a welcome and familiar sound, for it will be spoken in the words of his Son and will be the prayer of Christ himself. May the Father recognize in our prayer the words of his Son, and since he is the Advocate with the Father for our sins, let us make sure that when we sinners pray to the Father for forgiveness we use the words of our Advocate. For when he says: *Whatever you ask of the Father in my name, he will give it to you,* then surely our petition will be all the more powerful for being made not only in the name of Christ but also in the words of Christ's own prayer.

WEDNESDAY

A reading from the 'One Hundred Chapters on Spiritual Perfection' by Diadochus of Photice.
Cap. 12. 13. 14 : SC 90, 91

We must give our love to God alone

No one can love God if he is full of self-love. Anyone who really loves God mortifies his self-love for the sake of the superabundant treasures of grace that come from loving God. Once he has done this, such a man seeks only God's glory, never his own. The man given over to self-love seeks his own glory, but the man who loves God has the glory of his Maker at heart. Indeed the hallmark of a soul alive to the love of God is the delight it takes in its own abasement and its constant pursuit of God's glory by obedience to his every command. For because of his great majesty, glory belongs properly to God, but if he hopes to be admitted to God's friendship, it befits man to be humble. If we love God in this way and rejoice, like St John the Baptist, in the glory of the Lord, then we shall begin to say unceasingly : *He must be exalted, I must be humbled.*

I know someone who is so filled with the love of God — although he grieves because his love falls short of his desire to love — that his soul is entirely taken up with this burning desire for God to be glorified in him, and for his own total effacement. That man has not the slightest feeling of self-importance, even when he receives praise : the desire for abasement is so strong in him that the idea of standing on his dignity never crosses his mind. He celebrates the Liturgy as priests are bound to do, but so unswerving is he in his love for God that the abyss of this love swallows up all thought of his rank. His spirit of humility makes him quite oblivious of what could have been an occasion of vainglory, and his consequent desire for self-abasement prevents him from seeing himself as anything but an unprofitable servant, unfitted for his dignity. We should take such a man as our model, and fly every honour and distinction for the sake of the superabundant treasures of grace that come from loving him who has loved us so much.

The man who loves God in the depths of his heart has himself been loved by God, for the love anyone has for God depends upon how far his spiritual awareness enables him to perceive God's love for him. Once he has perceived it, his desire to live in the light of God's presence is so intense that it seems to penetrate his very bones; he loses all consciousness of himself, and is entirely transformed by the love of God. Such a man is in this life and at the same time not in it, for although he still lives in his body, he is constantly being taken out of himself in spirit by the love that carries him towards God. Henceforward he is united to God by the irresistible desire of a heart on fire with love, and for the sake of the love of God, he abandons his self-love for ever. *For if we have taken leave of our senses,* says the Apostle, *it is for the love of God : if we are in our right mind, it is for your sake.*

YEAR II

A reading from the Demonstrations on Circumcision by Aphraates the Persian.
Dem. 11, 11-12 : PS 1, 498-503.

Circumcision of the heart

The Law and the Covenant have been changed from beginning to end. In the first place God altered the covenant he had made with Adam, and made another with Noah. Again he made one with Abraham and later changed it in order to make another with Moses. And since Israel was not faithful to the Mosaic covenant, he finally made a covenant with the people of these last days, which will never be superseded.

With Adam the covenant was based on the prohibition against eating from the tree; with Noah it was the bow in the clouds; with Abraham, already singled out for his faith, God made a covenant of circumcision, to be a distinguishing mark and sign for his posterity. With Moses the covenant symbol was a lamb sacrificed on behalf of the people to celebrate the joy of the Passover. All these various covenants differed from each other.

The circumcision in which the Giver of covenants takes pleasure henceforward is the circumcision of the heart spoken of by Jeremiah. This is the covenant of faith, as sure and binding as the covenant God made with Abraham. He who gave this law cannot be rejected, either by those outside the (Mosaic) law or by those subject to it. For he gave Moses the law with its commandments and obligations; when the people did not obey it, he annulled it. Then he promised to give a new testament which, he said, would not be like the first, even though he was the author of both. The promised testament was that *all should know him from the least to the greatest*. There is no circumcision of the flesh here, nor sign of being a chosen people.

We know for certain, brethren, that God gives laws to different generations; they serve their purpose as long as it pleases him, and then he changes them. According to the apostle, the kingdom of God existed in the past in many and various ways in successive periods of time. Our God is true, and his covenants are absolutely trustworthy; this was so with each of the covenants in its day. Life and salvation are found by all who are circumcised in their hearts, and who then circumcise themselves a second time at the true Jordan, which is the sacrament of baptism for the remission of sins.

Joshua the son of Nun circumcised the people a second time with knives of flint when he crossed the Jordan with them. Jesus our Saviour circumcised the gentiles a second time, when those whose hearts were circumcised by faith in him were baptized and circumcised with the knife that is his word, sharper than any two-edged sword. Joshua, the son of Nun, led the people over to the promised land; Jesus our Saviour promises the land of life and salvation to all who have passed through the true Jordan and in faith have circumcised the foreskins of their hearts.

Blessed, therefore, are those whose hearts are circumcised and who are born again in the waters of the second circumcision; they are heirs with Abraham, the believing head and father of all peoples, whose faith was reckoned to him as righteousness.

THURSDAY

YEAR I

A reading from a Letter of St Fulgentius, bishop of Ruspe.
Epist. 14, 36-37; CCL 91, 429-431.

Christ is always living to intercede for us

Let us consider the ending we make to our prayers. We say 'through our Lord Jesus Christ, your Son', not 'through the Holy Spirit'. The Catholic Church does not make this distinction without reason, for it is founded on the mystery whereby *the man Christ Jesus, a priest for ever according to the order of Melchizedech, has been made the mediator between God and man, and through his own blood has entered once for all into the sanctuary; not indeed the man-made sanctuary which was only a copy of the true one*, but into heaven itself, where from his place at the right hand of God he makes intercession for us.

185

It was in regard to Christ's high-priestly office that the apostle said: *Through him let us continually offer a sacrifice of praise, the fruit of lips praising his name.* Through him, therefore, we offer our sacrifice of praise and supplication, because when we were God's enemies we were reconciled through the death of Christ. It is through him who stooped to become a sacrifice for us that our own sacrifice can find favour with God. This is why St Peter exhorts us to *be built like living stones into a spiritual house, to be a holy priesthood offering spiritual sacrifices pleasing to God through Jesus Christ,* and why we address God the Father 'through Jesus Christ our Lord'.

This reference to the priesthood surely points to the mystery of the Lord's incarnation, whereby the Son of God, *who was God by nature, emptied himself and took the form of a servant.* In this condition he humbled himself, becoming obedient unto death. Although he shared the Godhead equally with the Father, he was made less and *set a little below the angels.* For all that the Son remained the Father's equal, he was indeed made less when he lowered himself to assume the nature of man. But he made himself less when he emptied himself to accept the status of a slave. The lessening of Christ, then, was this very self-emptying, which was none other than the assumption of a servile condition.

Remaining God by nature, Christ is the Only-begotten Son, to whom with the Father we offer our sacrifices. When he assumed the nature of a slave, he became the priest through whom we are able to offer a living sacrifice which is holy and pleasing to God. However, no sacrifice could have been offered by us if Christ had not become a sacrifice for us, and if our very humanity had not become the true sacrifice of salvation in him. For when we make it clear that our prayers are offered through our Lord the eternal priest, we are acknowledging that he is truly our flesh and blood. This is what the apostle means by saying that *every high priest taken from among men is ordained to act on their behalf in relation to God, to offer gifts and sacrifices for their sins.* But when we say 'your Son' and add 'who lives and reigns with you in the unity of the Holy Spirit', we recall that unity of nature which is shared by Father, Son and Holy Spirit, and show at the same time that Christ himself, who is by nature one with the Father and the Holy Spirit, exercises the office of priesthood on our behalf.

YEAR II

A reading from the Paschal Homilies of St Cyril of Alexandria. Hom. 19, 2 : PG 77, 824-825.

For us the true lamb has been sacrificed

When the people of Israel were in Egypt they sacrificed a lamb in accordance with the instructions of Moses, who told them to eat it with unleavened bread and bitter herbs. As Scripture says, *You shall eat unleavened bread and bitter herbs for seven days.* Of course these are only types and symbols, for *we know that the law is spiritual* from its great master, St Paul. But what does St Paul mean by telling us that the law is spiritual if not that we ourselves are also bound by it? His words must certainly be true, for he had Christ within him and could not lie. Moreover, Christ himself said clearly : *Do not imagine that I have come to abolish the law or the prophets. I have not come to abolish them, but to fulfil them. I assure you that the law will not lose a single dot or stroke until its purpose is achieved. Heaven and earth will pass away, but my words will never pass away.*

We too must comply with the law then, but in what way? We have been called to achieve holiness through faith, but for us also a lamb has been sacrificed, the true lamb who takes away

187

the sin of the world. We are to accompany the eating of this sacrifice with spiritual food that is good, wholesome and most holy, the food that is typified in the law by unleavened bread, for we must interpret this in a spiritual way. Leaven, in the divinely inspired Scriptures, always signifies sin. Our Lord Jesus Christ warned his holy disciples to *beware of the leaven of the Scribes and the Pharisees.* Advisedly, Paul also wrote that people who have once been sanctified should put far from them the unclean leaven that corrupts mind and heart. *Get rid of the old yeast,* he urged, *and become freshly kneaded dough, unleavened as you are meant to be.*

Now we have been filled with a most wholesome desire for spiritual communion with Christ, the Saviour of us all. It is not only in our best interests therefore — it is also absolutely necessary that we should preserve purity of mind, be cleansed of all defilement, refrain from sin, and, in a word, free ourselves from every cause of contamination. Then, without blame, we shall enter into communion with Christ.

That we are also to eat bitter herbs with the sacrifice means that we must pass through bitter sufferings, and should appreciate the great value they possess. It would indeed be quite absurd for anyone desiring to serve God to imagine that we could achieve great virtue, and could glory in the supreme reward without having first contended for it, and given proof of the most steadfast courage. The approach to this goal is rugged and steep, and to most people it seems inaccessible. It becomes easy only for those whose desire to arrive is so strong that they are dismayed by nothing, and are ready to face hardship and toil. Christ's own words inspire them to do this: *Enter by the narrow gate,* he warned, *for the way to destruction is through a wide gate and along an easy road, and many are going that way. To attain to life you must pass through a narrow gate and go by a difficult road, and this road is found by only a few.*

FRIDAY

A reading from the Sermons of St Asterius of Amasea.
Hom. 13 : PG 40, 356, 361.

We must follow the Lord's example in caring for his flock

If, having been created in the image of God, we now desire to
resemble him, we must follow his example. The very name we
bear as Christians is proof of God's loving kindness towards
men. Let us, therefore, imitate the love of Christ. Consider and
wonder at the riches of his goodness. For when he was about to
show himself to men in man's own nature, he sent John ahead
of him to preach repentance, and before John he sent the
prophets to persuade men to change their way of life. Then he
came himself, and with his own voice he cried out : *Come to me,
all you who labour and are overburdened, and I will give you
rest.* And how did he receive those who listened to his call and
followed him? He readily forgave them their sins, in an instant
relieving them of all their cause for sorrow. The Word sanctified
them, the Spirit set his seal on them. The old man was buried in
the waters of baptism, the new man was born by grace. As a
result, enemies of God became his friends, strangers to him
became his sons, non-Christians became Christians, idolaters
learned to worship the true God.

It is for us now to follow our Lord's example in caring for
his flock. We should read the gospels carefully, for they are like
a mirror, showing us the pains he took and the kindness he
showed, and they will teach us how to be like him. Obscurely,
in the form of a parable, we see him there in the shepherd who
had a hundred sheep. When one of them became separated from
the flock and strayed, that shepherd did not remain with the

sheep that were still grazing with the others, but set out to look for the lost one. He crossed many chasms and ravines, he climbed over high mountains, he was almost overcome with exhaustion in the wilderness, and then, at last, he found his sheep.

When he had found it, he did not beat it, nor roughly drive it back into the fold, but instead he carefully carried it home on his own shoulders to restore it to the flock, and he was more delighted over this one sheep than over all the others.

Now there is a hidden meaning in this parable which we must try to penetrate; for the sheep is not really an animal, nor is the shepherd a man that cares for senseless beasts. No; he is someone very different. In fact, the purpose of this story is to reveal a sacred mystery, and its lesson for us is that we should not easily despair of men's salvation, nor should we abandon them when they are in peril. When they go astray, we are bound to search them out and bring them back to the fold. Then, when they return, we should be delighted to receive them into the fellowship of all right-living people.

YEAR II

A reading from the Mirror of Love, by the blessed abbot Aelred. Lib. 3, 5 : PL 195, 582.

Brotherly love must be modelled on the pattern given by Christ

The perfection of brotherly love consists in the love of our enemies, and to this there is no more powerful incentive than the grateful remembrance of Christ's own amazing patience. He who was *the fairest of the sons of men* offered his countenance to wicked men to spit upon; he permitted them to blindfold the eyes which see and rule the universe; he bared his back to the lash, and on his head, before which even angels bow, he endured the discomfort of the crown of thorns; he exposed himself to taunt and ridicule; and, last of all, still calm, unmoved and wholly unassuming, he faced the vinegar, the gall, the spear, the nails, the cross itself. *Like a sheep he was led to the slaughter, and like a lamb standing before the shearer he uttered no sound; he did not open his mouth.*

Only to hear the words *Father, forgive them,* spoken in a voice of infinite gentleness, love and peace, makes our hearts go out even to those who hate us. *Father,* he says, *forgive them;* could any prayer be more full of love and gentleness than this? Yet, even so, he found more to add to it. Not content simply to pray for those who did him ill, he was at pains to find excuses for them. *Father,* he said, *forgive them, for they have no idea what they are doing.* They do indeed sin enormously, yet they fail to see the full import of what they do. Hence, *Father, forgive them.* They nail him to the cross without a thought for who it is they are crucifying; for *had they but known, they would never have crucified the Lord of glory.* And so, *Father, forgive them.* To them he was just a breaker of the law, a usurper of divine prerogatives, one who had led the people astray. Therefore, the Lord says: *I have hidden my face from them, nor have they been allowed to recognize my glory;* and so, *Father, forgive them, for they have no idea what they are doing.*

To sum up, if a man would enjoy the perfection of brotherly love, he must embrace even his enemies within its bounds. But this divine fire may tend to lose its warmth in a hostile atmosphere, unless every man keeps before his eyes the unshakable patience of his loving Lord and Saviour.

SATURDAY

A reading from the fourth book of St Irenaeus 'Against Heresies'.
18, 1-2. 4. 5 : SC 100, 596-598. 606. 610-612.

The pure sacrifice offered by the Church

The oblation offered by the Church throughout the whole world,
in accordance with the Lord's instructions, is accounted by God
a pure and acceptable sacrifice. God has no need of sacrifice
from us, but it honours the man who offers it to have his gift
accepted. By a gift we show reverence and love for the King. It
should be offered, however, in all simplicity and innocence, for
we know the Lord's will in this regard from his own words:
*If you should remember, when you are offering your gift at the
altar, that your brother has a grievance against you, leave your
gift there, in front of the altar, go and be reconciled with your
brother first, and then come back and offer your gift.* We have
a duty, therefore, to offer God the first-fruits of his creatures.
This is the same teaching as Moses gave us when he said: *You
must not come into the Lord's presence empty-handed.* The man
who shows his gratitude to him by means of the very things that
have given him cause for this gratitude will himself receive
honour from God.

There has been no condemnation of the offering of sacrifice.
In former ages sacrifice was offered by the people of God; it is
still offered in the Church. Only the quality of the offering has
changed, now that the sacrifice is made by free men and not by
slaves. For although both have one and the same God, there is
a difference in kind between the offering of a slave and that of a
free man, since even sacrifice is meant to be a sign of a man's
freedom. In God's eyes, indeed, nothing is without import and
significance. So it is that whereas men formerly offered tithes to
God, those who have now been set at liberty place their whole

substance at the Lord's disposal, gladly and freely. They could offer no less, when they have the hope of receiving far more. The poor widow put into God's treasury all she had to live on.

We are bound, then, to offer sacrifice to him, and always to show our gratitude to the God who created us by making this offering of the first-fruits of his own creation with pure intention, genuine faith, firm hope, and heart-felt love. Only the Church offers the Creator this pure sacrifice. She takes it from among the works of his own hand, and she offers it to him with thanksgiving.

By offering God the things that are his, we make a fitting proclamation of the union and communion [of the Word with the body and blood of the Lord that is present in the Eucharist], and we profess our faith in the resurrection of flesh and spirit. For just as bread which comes from the earth is no longer ordinary bread after the consecration, but the Eucharist, which is composed of two elements, one earthly, the other heavenly, so also our bodies are no longer corruptible after receiving the Eucharist, but have the hope of resurrection.

YEAR II

A reading from the Pastoral Constitution on the Church in the Modern World.
Gaudium et Spes, 9-10.

Man's deeper questionings

Our world appears at once powerful and weak, capable of achieving the best or the worst; the way lies open to freedom or slavery, to advancement or slipping back, to brotherhood or hatred. Further, man is realizing that it is up to him to control properly the forces he has conjured up and which can either oppress him or serve his ends. Therefore he questions himself.

The strains under which the world labours today are connected with these more fundamental tensions. In man himself several elements are opposed. While as a creature he feels himself limited in several ways, at the same time he is aware of unlimited aspirations and of a call to a higher life. He is attracted by many things — he must always reject some and select others. Weak and sinful, he often does what he would prefer not to do and fails to do what he would like. He is divided against himself: from this it is that so many discords arise in society at large. Obviously, many who in practice live as materialists are distracted from this internal drama, or at least are hindered by extreme want from thinking about it. Many find refuge in various general theories about life. There are those who look forward to the full liberation of mankind by mere human effort, and are convinced that man's coming reign over the whole earth will satisfy all the desires of his heart. There are those who, themselves despairing of finding any meaning in life, praise the courage of men who deny life any general significance and dedicate themselves arbitrarily to self-fulfilment. None the less, in the face of present-day developments more and more people ask, or feel deeply the need of asking, absolutely fundamental questions: What is man? What is the meaning of pain, of evil, of death — things which persist in spite of so much progress? What are all our hard-won conquests worth? What can a man bring to society, what can he expect from it? What will come after life on earth?

The Church believes that Christ, who died and rose from the dead for all of us, gives man through his Spirit light and strength enough to live up to his high vocation; nor is there any other name under heaven given to men by which we must be saved. She believes that the key, the centre and purpose of all human history is to be found in her Lord and Master. The Church claims that beneath all change there are many things unchanging which have their ultimate foundation in Christ, who is the same yesterday and today and for ever.

SECOND SUNDAY OF LENT

YEAR I

A reading from the Commentary on the Gospel of St John by St Cyril of Alexandria.
Lib. 3, cap. 3 : PG 73, 428-433.

The mystery of Christ is revealed to us

I will raise up for them a prophet like yourself, one of their own race. I will put my words in his mouth, and he will speak to them as I command him. Anyone who will not listen to the words the prophet speaks in my name, I will punish.
Here, in the Book of Deuteronomy, which is a kind of review and summary of the Mosaic books, the mystery of Christ is again revealed to us by means of a subtle allegory, for we see in Moses the likeness of Christ. *For the Lord your God*, said Moses, *will raise up for you a prophet of your own race, like myself.*
Between God and the people of those days Moses was the appointed mediator; it was his task to help their infirmity by communicating to them the divine decrees. This again is only a symbol, but if we interpret it in terms of the reality which it foreshadows, it will teach us that Christ is the true Mediator between God and man. For our sake, Christ was born of a

195

woman, and he communicated to his disciples with a human voice the Father's will, which none but he knew or could declare; for in his nature as Son of the Father and as Wisdom he knows all things, even the depths of God.

The divine, the inexpressible glory of the supreme Being was beyond the power of mortal eyes to behold, pure and unveiled, for it is written, *No man can see my face and live.* Therefore, the Only-begotten Word of God had to share in our weakness, and in accordance with the mysterious designs of divine providence, to be clothed in a human body, for only in this way could he make known to us the divine will, the will of God the Father. As he himself said, *I make known to you all that I have heard from the Father,* and, *I have not spoken on my own authority; the Father who sent me has told me what to say and how to speak.*

So it is that Moses can be considered as a type of Christ, for by faithfully communicating the divine decrees to the people of Israel, he fulfilled the office of mediator. The mediation of Moses, however, was that of a mere servant, whereas the mediation of Christ is not only free but also deeply mysterious, for since Christ is by nature both divine and human, he is in intimate contact with those whom he reconciles. He is, so to speak, the bridge that restores communication between the human race and God the Father. Towards him the whole teaching of the law is orientated, for as Scripture says, Christ is the fulfilment of the law and the prophets.

A reading from Origen's Homilies on Exodus.
Hom. 5, 3-4; Edit. Maurist. t. 2, 145-146.

The way that leads to life is narrow and hard

Let us consider the path pointed out to Moses for his journey to the promised land. *From Etham*, the Lord said, *turn back and make your way between Pi-hahiroth and Migdol, which is opposite Baal-zephon.*

We might suppose a path pointed out by God to be a smooth and pleasant one, free of obstacles and requiring no effort from the traveller, but in fact God's way is an ascent, a tortuous and rugged climb. There can be no downhill road to virtue — it is uphill all the way, and the path is narrow and arduous. Listen also to the Lord's warning in the gospel: *The way that leads to life*, he says, *is narrow and hard.* Notice how close the agreement is between the gospel and the law. In the law the way of virtue is shown to be a tortuous climb; the gospels speak of the way that leads to life as narrow and hard. Is it not obvious then, even to the blind, that the law and the gospels were both written by one and the same Spirit?

This winding road, this ascent, has a watch-tower set over it. The ascent may be compared with works, the watch-tower with faith. We are thus shown the great difficulty and laborious effort involved in both faith and works, for many are the temptations we shall meet and many the obstacles to faith that lie in store for us in our desire to pursue the things of God.

Now when Pharaoh knew of their departure he said: 'The Israelites are wandering in the wilderness'. In the eyes of Pharaoh, obedience to God's commands leads us to wander in the wilderness because the way of wisdom is a tortuous route, rugged and winding.

Thus, when we profess our belief in one God, and in the same confession assert that Father, Son and Holy Spirit are one God, to unbelievers this seems difficult, incomprehensible and involved. Then, further, when we say that the Lord of majesty is also the son of man who descended from heaven and was crucified, these sayings are baffling and hard to understand. Whoever hears them and cannot respond to them with faith will say of believers: 'They are wandering in the wilderness'. But stand firm in your belief, cast aside all doubt, for we know that the way of faith has been laid down for us by God. Nor can we expect that the road to life will be a smooth one, free from trials. As St Paul warns: *All who wish to live a godly life in Christ will suffer persecution.* Yet for the man in search of the perfect life, better death on the road than failure even to set out on the quest.

YEAR A. Mt 17, 1-9

A reading from the Sermons of St Leo the Great.
Sermo 51, 3-4, 8. PL 54 : 310, 311, 313.

The Law was given by Moses : grace and truth have
come through Jesus Christ

In the presence of chosen witnesses the Lord unveils his glory, investing with such splendour that bodily appearance which he shares with the rest of men that his face shines like the sun and his clothes become white as snow.

The primary purpose of this transfiguration was to remove the scandal of the cross from the hearts of Christ's disciples; the greatness of his hidden glory was revealed to them to prevent their faith being shaken by the self-abasement of the suffering he was voluntarily to undergo. No less was the foresight that laid the foundations of the Church's hope, teaching the whole body of Christ the nature of the change it is to receive, and schooling his members to look forward to a share in the glory which had already shone forth in their head.

The Lord had told them of this when he spoke of his coming in majesty : *Then shall the just shine like the sun in the kingdom of their Father*. The blessed apostle Paul bears witness to the same thing : *I consider that the sufferings of this present time are not worth comparing with the glory that is to be revealed in us*. And again : *You have died, and your life is hidden with Christ in God. When Christ who is your life appears, then you also will appear with him in glory*.

Still further instruction was to come from the transfiguration to fortify the apostles and perfect their understanding. Moses and Elijah, representing the Law and the Prophets, appeared in conversation with the Lord. Thus through the presence of these five men the saying was fulfilled : *On the evidence of two or three witnesses every word shall stand*. What could be more firmly established than that Word in whose proclamation the trumpets of Old and New Testament sound in unison, and the writings of ancient witnesses are in perfect accord with the teaching of the gospel? The pages of both covenants agree with one another. He who had been promised beforehand by mysteriously veiled signs was now revealed clearly and distinctly in the radiance of his glory, since, as St John says, *the Law was given by Moses, but grace and truth have come through Jesus Christ*. In Christ what was promised by prophetic figures and what was signified by legal precepts are alike fulfilled, for by his presence he teaches the truth of the prophecies, and by grace he makes it possible for us to obey the commandments.

May we all, therefore, be confirmed in our faith through the preaching of the holy gospel, and let no one be ashamed of the cross by which Christ has redeemed the world. None of us must be afraid to suffer for the sake of justice or doubt the fulfilment of the promises, for it is through toil that we come to rest and through death that we pass to life. If we continue in the acknowledgement and love of Christ who took upon himself all the weakness of our lowly nature, what he conquered we shall conquer, and the promise he gave us we shall receive. So then, whether it is to encourage us to obey his commands or to endure hardships, let the Father's voice always be ringing in our ears and telling us : *This is my beloved Son, in whom I am well pleased : listen to him.*

YEAR B. Mk 9, 1-9

A reading from the Homilies of St Cyril of Alexandria.
Hom. IX In transfiguratione Domini : PG 77, 1011-1014.

Moses and Elijah spoke of how Jesus was to fulfil his destiny by dying in Jerusalem

Having gone up the mountain with three chosen disciples, Jesus was transfigured by a wonderful light so that even his clothes were seen to shine with bright radiance. Moses and Elijah stood near him, and together they spoke of how he was to fulfil his destiny by dying in Jerusalem. They spoke, that is to say, of the mystery of his incarnation, and of his saving passion upon the cross. For the law of Moses and the teaching of the holy prophets clearly foreshadowed the mystery of Christ. The law portrayed it by types and symbols inscribed on tablets. The prophets in many ways foretold that in his own time he would appear, clothed in human nature, and that for the salvation of all mankind, he would not refuse to suffer death upon the cross.

The presence of Moses and Elijah, and their speaking together, was meant to show unmistakably that the law and the prophets were the attendants of our Lord Jesus Christ. He was their Master, whom they had themselves pointed out in advance in prophetic words that proved their perfect harmony with one another. For the message of the prophets was in no way at variance with the precepts of the law.

At their appearance, Moses and Elijah did not keep silence; they spoke of how Jesus was to fulfil his destiny by dying in Jerusalem, they spoke of his passion and cross, and of the resurrection that would follow. Thinking, no doubt, that the time for the kingdom of God had already come, Peter would gladly have remained on the mountain. He suggested putting up three tents, without really knowing what he said. It was not yet time for the end of the world; nor was it in this present time that the hopes of the saints would be fulfilled — those hopes founded on Paul's promise that Christ *would transform our lowly bodies into the likeness of his glorious body.*

Only the initial stage of the divine plan had as yet been accomplished. Until its completion, was it likely that Christ, who came on earth for love of the world, would give up his wish to die for it? For his submitting to death was the world's salvation, and his resurrection was death's destruction.

As well as the vision of Christ's glory, wonderful beyond all description, something else occurred which was to serve as a vital confirmation, not only of the disciples' faith, but of ours as well. From a cloud on high came the voice of God the Father saying: *This is my Son, the Beloved, in whom I am well pleased. Listen to him.*

A reading from a Sermon on the Transfiguration of the Lord by Anastasius of Sinai.

Nn. 6-10 : Mélanges d'archéologie et d'histoire 67 (1955), 241-244.

It is good for us to be here

Upon Mount Thabor, Jesus manifested to his disciples a divine mystery. He had spoken to them during his public teaching about the Kingdom, and about his glorious Second Coming, but at first they may not perhaps have been completely convinced. Now, however, they were convinced inwardly beyond a shadow of doubt. Indeed, it was in order to confirm their faith in what lay in the future by its prefiguration in the present that Jesus granted them this wonderful vision upon Mount Thabor. It was as though he said to them : As time goes by, you may be in danger of losing your faith. My desire is to save you from this, and therefore I tell you now, at the present moment, that *some of you standing here will not taste death until you see the Son of Man coming* in the glory of his Father. Moreover, in order to assure us that Christ could command such power when he wished, the evangelist continues : *Six days later, Jesus took with him Peter, James and John, and led them up a high mountain where they were alone. There, before their eyes, he was transfigured. His face shone like the sun, and his clothes became white as light. Then the disciples saw Moses and Elijah appear, and they were talking to Jesus.*

These are the divine wonders that we celebrate today; this vision on the mountain is for us now both a revelation and our salvation; this is the festival of Christ that has drawn us here. These mysteries are holy beyond all telling. We should long to enter into them in company with those specially chosen from among the inspired messengers of God's word. Let us listen to

God's most holy voice calling us together so compellingly from above, as though from the top of a mountain. Jesus goes before us to show us the way, both up the mountain and into heaven. I am bold enough to say that we should follow him with all speed in our desire for the heavenly vision that will give us a share in his radiance; for that vision will renew our spiritual nature and transform us into his own likeness, making us for ever sharers in his Godhead, and raising us to heights as yet undreamt of.

Let us run, confident and full of joy, to enter into the cloud, to become like Moses and Elijah, like James and John. Let us be caught up like Peter to behold the divine vision, and to be transfigured by that glorious transfiguration. We must retire from the world, stand aloof from the earth, rise above the body, detach ourselves from creatures and turn to the Creator, to whom Peter in ecstasy exclaimed: *Lord, it is good for us to be here.*

It is good indeed, Peter, for us to be here with Jesus, and to remain here for ever. What could be happier or more sublime, what honour could be greater than to be with God, to be like him, and to live in his light?

Therefore, since each of us possesses God in his heart and is being transformed into his divine image, we also should cry out with transports of joy: *It is good for us to be here* — here where all things shine with divine radiance, where there is joy and gladness and exultation; where everything within our hearts is peaceful, serene, and still; where God is seen. For here, in our hearts, Christ takes up his abode, together with the Father. He approaches and says: *Today salvation has come to this house.* With Christ, our hearts receive all the riches of his eternal blessings, and there, where they are stored up for us in him, we see reflected as in a mirror both the first-fruits and the whole of the world to come.

MONDAY

A reading from the Pastoral Constitution on the Church in the Modern World.
Gaudium et Spes, 48.

The holiness of marriage and the family

Man and woman, who by the conjugal pact are *no longer two but one*, help and minister to each other in an intimate linking of their persons and activities; they experience the real meaning of their union and achieve it more every day. This intimate union of two persons giving themselves to each other demands their full fidelity and argues for their indissoluble unity; so does the good of their children.

Christ our Lord abundantly blessed this manifold love which springs from the source of divine charity and forms a union on the model of his own union with his Church. For just as God once encountered his people in a covenant of love and trust, so now as the Saviour of the world and the Spouse of the Church he encounters faithful spouses in the sacrament of Christian marriage. Moreover, he remains with them; just as he loved the Church and gave himself up for it, so do married partners, by a mutual surrender, love each other with a lasting fidelity. Full conjugal love is taken up into divine love, guided and enriched by the redemptive virtue of Christ and the Church's saving action. Thus, married people are effectively led to God and helped and strengthened in the sublime function of a father or a mother. Christian married people are fortified in the dignity of their state, and consecrated to its duties by a special sacrament. Carrying out their conjugal and family functions by virtue of this, penetrated by the Spirit of Christ who fills their lives with faith, hope and charity, they make steady progress towards their own perfection and mutual sanctification and give glory to God in unison.

Children, and indeed all those living in a family circle, will, by parents' example and by family prayer, more easily find the way of salvation and holiness. Parents clothed with the dignity and office of fathers and mothers will diligently carry out the task of education which is first and foremost theirs, especially that of religious upbringing.

Children, as living members of a family, contribute in their own way to the sanctification of their parents. They will respond with gratitude and affection, devotion and trust to the benefits they receive from their parents, and, as children should, they will remember their parents' needs in time of trouble or in the loneliness of old age.

YEAR II

A reading from the Catecheses of St John Chrysostom.
Cat. 3, 24-27 : SC 50, 165-167.

Moses and Christ

The Jews witnessed miracles, but you shall witness miracles too, greater and more glorious miracles than those they saw on their departure from Egypt. You did not see the drowning of Pharaoh and his armies, but you have seen the overwhelming of the devil and all his legions. The Jews passed through the sea : you have passed through death. They were delivered from the Egyptians : you have been freed from devils. They escaped from slavery to heathens : you have escaped the far more grievous slavery to sin.

Would you learn in other ways how much more highly you were prized? The Jews of those days could not look upon the glorified face of Moses, even though he was their fellow-servant, and one of their own race; but you have seen the face of Christ in his glory. As Paul exclaims, *We behold the glory of the Lord with no veil covering our faces.* The Jews had Christ to accompany them then, but we even more certainly have him with us now. The Lord accompanied them out of his good-will towards Moses: he accompanies us not simply in virtue of his good-will towards our bishop, who is to us as Moses was to them, but also because of your obedience. For them, after Egypt there was the desert: for you at your departure from this life there will be heaven. They had in Moses the best possible guide and commander: we too have our Moses to lead and command us — God himself.

What was the distinguishing mark of their Moses? Scripture says that he was *a very humble man, the most humble man on earth.* This we can truly say of our Moses, for he had with him the most gentle Spirit, with whom in his very being he is one. The Moses of those days raised his hands to heaven and brought down manna, the bread of angels, but our Moses raises his hands to heaven and brings us food for everlasting life. The other Moses struck the rock and brought forth streams of water; our Moses touches the altar, strikes the heavenly table, and makes the fountains of the Spirit gush forth. To enable the flocks to gather round from all sides and to drink from its saving waters, the altar is placed, like a fountain, in the middle.

Since, then, we have before us such a life-giving fountain, and this table affords us countless blessings, innumerable graces, let us approach with genuine faith and purity of conscience to receive the grace and mercy that will help us in time of need. This we can do through the grace and mercy of the only-begotten Son of God, our Lord and Saviour Jesus Christ, through whom and with whom be glory, honour and power to the Father and the life-giving Spirit now and always and for endless ages. Amen.

TUESDAY

A reading from 'The Adoration and Worship of God in Spirit and in Truth' by St Cyril of Alexandria.
Lib. 8 : PG 573-576.

Moses and the Law have been superseded, and Christ has become our guide

In many ways there is in the Old Testament a real foreshadowing of the mystery of Christ, and a certain prefiguration of his saving passion, which has freed us from all that had power to harm us, and to plunge us into evils from which there was no escape.

One example was the remission of debts at the end of every seventh year, pointing towards the time of universal remission of sins. Another was the law that no one should give or receive more than forty strokes of the scourge, signifying the eagerly awaited time when the only-begotten Son would become incarnate, and we should be healed by his wounds. When the leaders of Israel insulted him and Pilate ordered him to be scourged, he was made weak on account of our sins, but we were delivered from punishment. In the past sinners were frequently scourged, but Christ suffered punishment for our sake. Just as he died for all mankind, so he was scourged for all, since he by himself was a worthy ransom for the whole human race. By allowing no more than forty strokes of the scourge, the law foreshadowed the time when Christ's coming would bring remission of sins and the end of all punishment, for beneath symbols there lies the beauty of truth.

We must know also that after the Israelites had offended him, God swore an oath that he would not lead them into the promised land, and they spent forty years wandering in the wilderness. At the end of that time, however, he relented, and their descendants were able to cross the Jordan to enter the promised land. God's anger lasted for forty years and no longer. The fact that a man received up to forty strokes of the scourge is thus a clear symbol of the remission of sins after the lapse of forty years. This remission brings us to the spiritual crossing of the Jordan, and to the stone knives that signify spiritual circumcision. It places us under the command of Jesus, for Moses and the law have been superseded, and Christ has become our guide.

YEAR II

A reading from St Augustine's Commentary on the Psalms.
Ps. 140, 4-6; CCL 40, 2028-2029.

Christ's whole body shares in his passion

I have called to you, Lord; make haste to help me! We are all in a position to make these words our own. Yet if I pronounce them, they will not be uttered by myself alone, but by Christ in his totality. They are spoken in the name of his Body; for while he was on earth he prayed as one who shared our human nature, he besought the Father in the name of all his members, and during his prayer drops of blood were forced from every pore of his body. That is what Scripture tells us: *Jesus prayed with such earnestness that his sweat became like drops of blood.* This bleeding of his entire body surely signifies that the whole Church will bleed with the suffering of martyrs.

I have called to you, Lord; make haste to help me! Hear my voice when I cry out to you. Certainly you could not have thought that once you had said 'I have called to you', you would have no further need for prayer. You may have cried out, but do not suppose you are safe. When your suffering is over, then

208

your cries may cease. But if we believe that the Church, Christ's body, is liable to suffering until the end of time, then must we not only say : *I have called to you; make haste to help me*, but add with the Psalmist : *hear my voice when I cry to you.*

Let my prayer rise up before you like incense; let the raising of my hands be like an evening sacrifice. Every Christian is aware that this passage is usually understood of Christ our head. For, as evening drew near, the Lord yielded up his soul upon the cross in the certainty of receiving it back again; it was not wrested from him against his will. But we too are surely also represented here. He had nothing to hang upon the cross except the body he had received from us. And it was surely not possible for God the Father to abandon his only Son, who shared with him the one Godhead. Nevertheless, when he nailed our human weakness to the cross — that cross to which, as the apostle says, *our unregenerate nature has been fastened along with him* — it was with the voice of our humanity that he exclaimed : *My God, my God, why have you forsaken me?*

That, then, is the evening sacrifice : the Lord's own passion, his cross, the offering on it of the saving Victim, of that holocaust which is acceptable to God. And by his rising, Christ has turned that evening sacrifice into a morning oblation.

Similarly, the pure prayer which ascends from a faithful heart will be like incense rising from a hallowed altar. No fragrance can be more pleasing to God than that of his Son's own prayer; may the prayers of all the faithful breathe out the same perfume.

Our unregenerate nature — it is the apostle who speaks once more — *has been fastened to the cross along with him, in order that our sin-stained humanity may be renewed and cleansed, and we ourselves may no longer be slaves to sin.*

WEDNESDAY

A reading from a Sermon of St Bernard on the Song of Songs.
Sermon 61 : 3-5. Opera omnia 2, 156-157.

Where sins abounded, grace was even more abundant

Where is there a safe, firm refuge for man in his helplessness except in the wounds of the Saviour? The more powerful he is to save, the more securely will I dwell there. The world may rage, my body may be a burden to me, the devil may lie in wait, yet I do not fall; I am founded on a rock. I have sinned and my sin is great; my conscience is troubled, but I will not despair for I call to mind the wounds of my Lord. *He was pierced through for our faults.* What can be so close to death that it cannot be freed by the death of Christ? When I remember how powerful and effective a remedy I have, I can no longer fear even the most deadly disease.

Therefore the man who says: 'My sin is so great that I cannot be forgiven' is wrong. It could only be true if he were not a Christian and Christ's merits did not apply to him. But a member of Christ can claim as his own what belongs to the head. As for me, I unhesitatingly claim for my own all that I need from the heart of our Lord, taking from him what is lacking in myself; his mercies overflow and they have many outlets, for they have pierced his hands and his feet, they have opened his side with a lance. Through this rock that is cleft *I can draw honey, and oil from the hardest stone* — that is, I can *taste and see that the Lord is sweet.* His thoughts were thoughts of peace, and I did not know it, for *who could ever know the mind of the Lord? Who could ever be his counsellor?* But the nail that penetrates has become a key that unlocks the Lord's will for me. Let me look more closely. The nails and the wounds proclaim that *God is in Christ, reconciling the world to himself. The iron pierced his soul, it entered his heart,* so that now he must know and understand my suffering. The secret of his heart lies bare, the wounds of his body lie bare, that great mystery of his love is revealed, and with it *the tender mercy of our God, who visits us like the dawn from on high.* For where can we see more clearly than through his wounds his gentleness, humility and abundant mercy shining forth? No man can have greater love than this, to lay down his life for slaves or condemned criminals.

My merit is the Lord's mercy. Surely I shall not be without merit so long as he is not without mercy? But if the mercies of the Lord are manifold, then I am rich in merits. If I am conscious of a multitude of sins, yet it is true that *where sins abounded grace was even more abundant.* If *the Lord's love for those who fear him lasts for all eternity, I,* too, *will sing your love for ever.* I shall not sing my own praises: *I will celebrate your righteousness, Lord, for righteousness is your alone.* That same righteousness is also mine, for God has made you my justification.

YEAR II

A reading from 'The Adoration and Worship of God in Spirit and in Truth' by St Cyril of Alexandria.
Lib. 3 : PG 68, 275-278.

The triumphs of Christ

When Moses had climbed the hill to watch the battle and to see how Joshua fared, he raised his hands, and whenever he did so the Israelites had the advantage, but they fell back if he lowered them, and then Amalek pressed home the attack.

Now the outstretched hands of Moses are clearly a symbol of the cross, and they show us that if we consider it an honour to

211

resemble Christ and to share in his reproach, which is his glorious cross, no enemy, however firmly bent on our destruction, not even the devil himself, will have power to overcome us — we, like the Israelites, shall be invincible.

Scripture tells us that because the arms of Moses grew heavy and it was hard for him to keep them raised, *they took a stone and put it under him, and he sat on it, while Aaron and Hur stood on either side of him holding up his arms.* Now this stone is Christ, for he is *the cornerstone, chosen and precious.* Those of the sons of Israel who are better disposed and more ready to learn, the remnant chosen by grace, rest upon him and stretch out their arms in acceptance of the cross, knowing that Christ himself strengthens and supports them. For since Christ is at once both judge and high priest, he is also prefigured in Aaron and Hur. It is he who held together the remnant of Israel so that they could be saved by faith. This must surely be the meaning of the prophetic words of Isaiah: *If the Lord of hosts had not left us a remnant, we should have been like Sodom and Gomorrah.*

After the overthrow of Amalek, the Lord said to Moses: *Record this in a book and read it to Joshua.* He gave this order because the triumphs of Christ were also to be recorded by the holy evangelists as an everlasting remembrance. The reason the book was to be read to Joshua is that the lives of the saints are really an offering of praise and honour to Christ.

When Amalek had been conquered, Moses built an altar to God, and engraved on it the name: *My Lord is my refuge.* This is another image of Christ who became our Lord and refuge when he conquered the ruler of this world, destroyed the power of death, and for our sake offered himself to God the Father as a victim without blemish and as a sweet-smelling sacrifice. The altar of Moses was, therefore, a symbol of Christ, for his name is in all truth, *My Lord is my refuge.*

THURSDAY

A reading from the Sermons of John Mediocris, Bishop of Naples.
Sermo 18 : PLS 4, 785-786.

Love the Lord and walk in his ways

The Lord is my light and my salvation : whom shall I fear? How great a servant of the Lord was the Psalmist who knew the manner of that illumination and its source, and the nature of the one on whom the light was shed. He perceived the light — not the light of the sun moving towards evening, but that other light, *which the eye does not see.* Souls enlightened by this light do not rush blindly into sin, nor stumble into evil ways.

When our Lord said : *Walk while you have the light among you,* what light did he mean but himself? Did he not say : *I have come as light into the world,* so that those with sight may become blind, and the blind may see the light? That same Lord, then, is our light, the sun of justice, by whose light his Church throughout the world has been illumined; and it was of him that the prophet was speaking figuratively when he cried : *The Lord is my light and my salvation : whom shall I fear?*

The man with this light in his soul does not waver, nor does he abandon the path; he is ready to endure every hardship. Discerning his true home from afar, he bears with difficulties, is not cast down by the problems of life, but finds his strength in God; he keeps his emotions in check and is able to persevere; he draws patience from his humility. That true light which *enlightens every man coming into the world* gives himself to those who fear him. On those he chooses, when he chooses, the Son sheds his radiance. To whom he will he reveals himself.

When the light dawns on a man who is *sitting in darkness and the shadow of death* — in the darkness of evil and the shadow of sin — this man is appalled at himself. He takes stock, repents and is ashamed, saying: *The Lord is my light and my salvation : whom shall I fear?* A great salvation indeed, my brethren; a salvation that fears no weakness, dreads no weariness, heeds no sorrow. We should then cry aloud with all our might, not only from our lips but from our heart: *The Lord is my light and my salvation : whom shall I fear?* If it is he who enlightens, he who saves, whom indeed shall I fear? Let them come, those promptings of darkness: *the Lord is my light.* They may come, but they can have no effect; they may assail our heart, but they cannot overthrow it. Let them come, those blinding passions: *the Lord is my light.* He is our strength, who gives himself to us as we give ourselves to him.

YEAR II

A reading from a treatise on the Psalms by St Hilary of Poitiers. Ps. 127, 1-3; CSEL 24, 628-630.

What is meant by the fear of God

Blessed are those who fear the Lord and walk in his ways. We should note that whenever mention is made in Scripture of the fear of God, it is never proposed to us in isolation, as though it were sufficient on its own account for the crowning of our faith; it is always preceded or followed by many other things from which the meaning and perfection of the fear of the Lord can be understood. This is made clear by Solomon's own words in his Book of Proverbs: *Only after you have invoked wisdom and called upon knowledge, sought them out like silver and tracked them down like hidden treasure, will you discover what is meant by the fear of God.* Thus we see that to reach a proper understanding of the fear of God we must first pass through a number of preliminary stages. For before we can reach it we must call upon wisdom and dedicate ourselves to serious study. Wisdom must not only be sought out, but also, when found, keenly scrutinised. For only thus can we come to a genuine understanding of what is meant by the fear of God. Nor should our estimate of what is meant by fear be that of ordinary men.

Fear is that feeling which a defenceless human being will experience when he knows that in all probability he must submit to some form of suffering he would far sooner be without. For instance, we are disturbed by the consciousness of our own guilt, by the claims of those who have power over us, by the force those stronger than ourselves are able to exert against us, by our liability to illness, by our defencelessness before the onslaught of untamed nature, or by our exposure to every kind of evil and disaster. Such fear as this need not be taught us by anyone, since all who share our feeble human nature are instinctively aware of it; the very things we fear themselves strike terror into us.

But it has been written concerning the fear of the Lord : *Come now, my sons, give ear to me, and I will instruct you in the fear of God.* The fear of God is therefore capable of being learnt; it is something that can and must be taught us. It is not aroused in us by the experience of terror, but is built up within us by means of reasoned and calm instruction. Nor does our natural timidity cause it to dwell in us, but we gradually develop it through our observance of God's laws, our effort to live a blameless life, our striving after truth.

For us, the fear of God is closely linked with love, and perfect love absorbs it altogether. For if we have true love for God, then it will be love, not fear, that will impel us to observe his laws, respect his statutes, and trust in his promises. Listen to what

Scripture has to say about this: *So now, Israel, what does God ask of you other than to fear the Lord your God and walk in all his ways, keeping his commandments faithfully and loving him with all your heart and soul, in order that all may go well with you?*

The ways of the Lord indeed are many, though it is he who is The Way. (He made this claim to be The Way when speaking of himself, and he justified it by saying: *No man can reach the Father except through me*.) Therefore we must explore a number of different ways and examine them from every angle; we must carefully consider everything our teachers say to us about them, if we are to discover the one good way that leads to eternal life. Such ways are found in the Law and the Prophets, in the Epistles and Gospels, and in the various works of spiritual masters; those who follow ways like these and walk along them in the fear of God, will certainly come at last to eternal bliss.

FRIDAY

YEAR I

A reading from St John Fisher's Treatise concerning the Fruitful Sayings of David in the Seven Penitential Psalms.
Psalm CI.

The wonderful mercy of God

He has looked down from his high sanctuary. Since even after the great and innumerable benefits bestowed on us by our merciful Lord we fall continually into every sin and wretchedness, we can truly say that our utter sinfulness has removed us so far from him that it is a wonder he will consent to look so far down to us in our ungratefulness towards his loving mercy.

For it was his mercy that brought the people of Israel out of Egypt in such a marvellous way, with so many signs and wonders, causing them to walk dry-shod through the Red Sea. His mercy, too, sent down from heaven angels' food, and wild fowl, curlews and quails. His mercy caused water to flow out of the hard stone for their relief, gave them victory over all their enemies, and made the waters of the Jordan leave their natural course and turn backward. By his mercy he divided and shared out the Promised Land, according to the number of the tribes and families of Israel ordained to possess it. He had mercy on them again and again after they had committed idolatry. In his mercy he also called us to grace, who naturally were of the seed of the gentiles, and grafted us in the true olive-tree of faith, suffering its natural boughs to be cut away — the olive-tree signifying the people of the Jews. Lastly, he spared not his own Son, but gave him up in redemption for us all. And in spite of that, in our persistent sinfulness, we are heedless of it, not reflecting upon the love of God towards us; but, forgetful of the great merits of our merciful Lord, we sinners are too proud to follow in his footsteps.

O tough and steely hearts! O hearts more hard than flint or other stone! O great wretchedness in which we have removed ourselves so far away from God that it is a wonder of wonders to know that he looks down upon such extreme ingratitude! Therefore, let these marvellous benefits of God be written for a continual remembrance to all Christian people who shall come after us, *because he has looked down from his high sanctuary*. We will record this goodness of God and have it in eternal remembrance, to the intent that all who live after us may recount to each other how merciful our Lord has been — so merciful, indeed, that his mercy cannot be expressed in words.

A reading from the fourth book of St Irenaeus 'Against Heresies'
16, 2-5 : SC 100, 564-572.

The Lord's Covenant

In the book of Deuteronomy, Moses addresses the people saying :
*At Horeb the Lord your God made a covenant, a covenant not
with your forefathers, but with you.* Why did the Lord make no
covenant with their forefathers? Because *the law is not meant
for people of upright life,* and their forefathers were good men
who had the virtues of the Decalogue inscribed in their hearts
and souls. They loved the God who created them, and were
guilty of no injustice towards their neighbour. Through their
own integrity they lived according to the law, and did not need
the warning of a written code.

But when this sense of justice and this love for God was
forgotten, and in Egypt altogether ceased to exist, God was
forced by his great love for men to make himself known by the
sound of a voice. By his own power he brought the people out
of Egypt in the hope that men would once again submit themselves to his guidance. To teach those who disobeyed him not to
despise their Creator, he punished them. He fed the people with
manna for their spiritual nourishment. As Moses says in Deuteronomy, *He fed you with manna, which had been unknown to
your fathers, and he did this to make you realize that man does
not live by bread alone, but by every word that proceeds from
the mouth of God.*

God commanded man to love him; he taught him to treat his
neighbour with justice. By the Ten Commandments, which were
intended to preserve man from sin and from being unworthy of
him, God prepared man to live in friendship with himself and in
harmony with his neighbour, all of which was simply for man's

own good, for God needed nothing from man. It conferred great glory on man, for it gave him what he had been deprived of before, namely, friendship with God; but it did not benefit God, for God stood in no need of man's love. The need was all on man's side because he lacked the glory of God, and could receive it only by obedience to him. This is why Moses urged the people: *Choose life, so that you and your descendants may live. Love the Lord your God, obey his voice and cling to him, for that will mean life for you, and length of days.*

To prepare man for that life, the Lord himself gave the commands of the Decalogue to all alike, and they remain in force today. Their meaning has been extended and amplified, but they have not been annulled. On the other hand, the precepts appropriate for the education and correction of the people of Israel in their state of servitude the Lord delivered separately, through Moses. As Moses himself says: *At that time the Lord commanded me to teach you statutes and decrees.*

Those precepts, therefore, which were given them as a sign of their servitude, he has annulled by the New Covenant of freedom; but the precepts of the natural law which befit free men and are meant for all, he has strengthened and amplified by his bounty in freely making us his sons by adoption, so that we should know him as our Father, love him with our whole heart, and unswervingly follow his Word.

SATURDAY

A reading from the Pastoral Constitution on the Church in the Modern World.
Gaudium et Spes, 18, 22.

The mystery of death

It is in the face of death that the riddle of human existence becomes most acute. Man suffers not only from pain or the slow breaking-down of his body, but also from the terror of perpetual extinction. It is a sound instinct that makes him recoil and revolt at the thought of this total destruction, of being snuffed out. He is more than matter, and the seed of eternity he bears within him rebels against death. All technical undertakings, however valuable, are powerless to allay man's anxiety; prolonging his span of life here cannot satisfy the desire for a future life inescapably rooted within him.

While all imagination fails us in the face of death, the Church appeals to revelation in telling man he is created by God, for blessedness, beyond the wretchedness of this life. The Christian faith teaches that bodily death, from which man would have been delivered had he not sinned, will yet be conquered because the almighty and merciful Saviour will give back to man the salvation he lost through his own fault. God called man and still calls him to an eternal imperishable communion of his whole nature with the divine life. This is the victory Christ gained in rising from the dead, since by dying himself he freed man from death. To any thinking man, then, to offer faith supported by solid reasons is to offer an answer to his anxieties about his future destiny. At the same time it is to offer him the means of communion in Christ with his loved ones already dead, since faith gives hope that they have attained true life with God.

Certainly the need and duty of battling against evil through many trials presses on the Christian, and the need of undergoing death; but he shares in the paschal mystery, becomes like Christ in his death and will encounter the resurrection fortified with hope.

Nor does this hold only for those who believe in Christ: it holds for all men of good will in whose hearts grace works in an invisible fashion. Christ died for everybody; everybody's ultimate vocation is the same divine vocation; then we must hold that the Holy Spirit offers everybody the possibility of sharing in some way known to God in this paschal mystery.

Such is the mystery of man as the Christian revelation expounds it to believers. Through Christ and in Christ, then, light is shed on the riddles of pain and death which, considered apart from the gospel, overwhelm us. Christ rose, by his death destroying death, giving us abundant life, so that as sons united in the Son we can cry out in the Spirit, *Abba, Father !*

YEAR II

A reading from the Treatise of St Ambrose on Flight from the World.
Chapter 6, 36; (7), 44; 8, 45; 9, 52. CSEL 32, 192, 198-199, 204.

Let us cleave to God, our one true good

Where a man's heart is, there is his treasure, and this treasure our Lord will certainly not deny to those who pray for it. Since the Lord is generous, especially to those who hope in him, let us cling to him, let us belong to him with all our heart, with all our soul and with all our strength, so that we may live always in his light and see his glory, and be rewarded by the grace of heavenly joy. We should raise our minds to this supreme good, we should live in it, we should cling to it, for this is the good that is beyond the reach of every mind, beyond the grasp of every intelligence, the good that enjoys perpetual peace and tranquility — peace that surpasses all understanding and lies beyond perception.

This is the good that penetrates all being. We all of us live in it, and on it our lives depend, but it depends on nothing, has nothing higher than itself, for it is divine. No one is good but God alone, therefore what is good is divine, and what is divine is good. That is why it is written: *From your generous hand they shall all be filled with good.* It is through the goodness of God that we receive all good things in the universe as our due, and these good things are mixed with nothing evil. They are the good things that Scripture promises to the faithful, saying: *You shall eat the good things of the earth.*

We died with Christ, we carry his death with us in our body so that Christ's life in us may be made known to the whole world. It is no longer our life that we live but Christ's life, a life of innocence, a life of chastity, a life of simplicity and of every virtue. With Christ we have risen from the dead, in him we live, in him we ascend, so that the serpent seeking to wound our heel looks in vain for us on earth.

Let us fly from this place, for you can fly in spirit even though you are held back in body. You can be here and in our Lord's presence at the same time if you cling to him in your soul and follow him in your thoughts; if you walk in his ways by faith and not by sight; if you fly to him, for he is our refuge and our strength, and of him David has said: *I sought refuge in God and he did not fail me.*

If only we could fly to God who is our refuge in heaven and above the heavens, for then we should find peace, rest from labour, and feasting at that great Sabbath of which Moses said: *The sabbath of the land will itself feed you.* To rest in God, to

222

see and taste his beauty will be as delightful as a banquet, full of joy and peace.

Let us hasten like deer to springs of water. Let our souls thirst as David thirsted. If you would know what that fountain is, listen to the words of David: *You are the fountain of life.* This is the fountain to which my soul must say: *When shall I go to see the face of God?* For the fountain is God himself.

THIRD SUNDAY OF LENT

YEAR I

A reading from the Homilies of St John Chrysostom on the Letter to the Hebrews.
Hom. 2, 3 : PG 63, 23, 24-25.

Though he was Lord and God, he did not refuse
to assume the condition of a slave

The Son of God sustains the whole universe by his word of power. In the beginning God said *Let there be light.* But here we see that the Son also acts by the power of his word, *sustaining the whole universe,* controlling and supporting what would otherwise disintegrate. The preservation of the world is, in fact, no less a task than its creation. If so bold a statement may be allowed, it is even greater, for in the one instance something is produced from nothing, while in the other created things are preserved from falling apart and returning to non-existence. This is indeed a great and wonderful work, a proof of immense power.

In saying that *he sustains the whole universe*, therefore, Scripture is telling us that the Lord makes light of the great burden of creation; it is no effort to him, for, the text adds, he does it *by his word of power*. Yes, truly: *by his word*. We indeed may think of a word as something insubstantial, but Scripture shows us that it is not so with God. The expression used in the Letter to the Hebrews: *he sustains the whole universe by his word of power*, has the same significance as St John's message: *In him was life*. Both indicate the power of the Word to preserve his creation, since he is himself the life of the whole universe.

The text continues: *In his own person he has made purification for our sins*. Thus, after speaking of these great and wonderful matters, Scripture goes on to describe God's providential care for men. *He sustains the whole universe* is, indeed, an all-embracing statement; but the continuation is greater still and no less all-embracing, since the salvation offered to all men comes through the Son of God. Moreover, when John had pointed out God's providence in the words *In him was life*, he went on to say *And in him was light*. The same declaration is made here to the Hebrews: *When he had made purification for our sins, he took his seat at the right hand of the Majesty on high*. Here we are given two signs of God's care for us: we are cleansed from sin, and this is brought about through the Son of God himself. How many texts there are that glory not only in our reconciliation with God but in its accomplishment through his Son! So immense a gift becomes even greater when it is given us through him.

Now when Scripture says that *after making purification for our sins, he took his seat* at God's right hand, it recalls the cross to our minds and then proceeds at once to teaching on the resurrection and ascension.

Since we know these things, therefore, let us be neither

ashamed nor presumptuous. He who was Lord and God and Son of God did not refuse to assume the condition of a slave; surely then we ought to embrace every task that is laid upon us, no matter how humble and lowly it may be.

YEAR II

A reading from the Treatise of St Bernard on the Degrees of Humility and Pride.
III, 6 : Edit. critica, Rome 1963, t. 3, 20-21.

We cannot have compassion on the weakness of
others until we first recognize our own

Knowledge of the truth comprises three degrees, which I will try to set out as briefly as possible.

In the first place we seek truth in ourselves; then we seek it in our neighbour, and last of all we search for truth in its own essential nature. We discover truth in ourselves when we pass judgment on ourselves; we find it in our neighbour when we suffer in sympathy with him; we search out its own nature by contemplation in purity of heart. Notice not only the number of these degrees, but also their order. Before we inquire into the nature of truth, Truth itself must first teach us to seek it in our neighbour. Then we shall understand why, before we find it in our neighbour, we must seek it in ourselves. The sequence of Beatitudes given in the Sermon on the Mount places the merciful before the pure in heart. The merciful are those who are quick to see truth in their neighbour; they reach out to him in compassion and identify with him in love, responding to the joys and sorrows in the lives of others as if they were their own. They make themselves weak with the weak, and burn with indignation when others are led astray. They are always ready to share the joys of those who rejoice and the sorrows of those who mourn.

Men whose inner vision has thus been cleansed by the exercise of brotherly love can delight in the contemplation of truth in itself, for it is love of truth which makes them take upon themselves the misfortunes of others. But can people find the truth in their neighbour if they refuse to support their brothers in this way; if on the contrary they either scoff at their tears or disparage their joy, being insensitive to all feelings but their own? There is a popular saying which well suits them: A healthy man cannot feel the pains of sickness, nor a well-fed man the pangs of hunger. The more familiar a man is with sickness or hunger, the greater will be his compassion for others who are sick or hungry.

For just as pure truth can only be seen by the pure in heart, so the sufferings of our fellow men are more truly felt by hearts that know suffering themselves. However, we cannot sympathize with the wretchedness of others until we first recognize our own. Then we shall understand the feelings of others by what we personally feel, and know how to come to their help. Such was the example shown by our Saviour, who desired to suffer himself in order to learn to feel compassion, and to be afflicted in order to learn how to show mercy. Scripture says of him that he learned the meaning of obedience through what he suffered. In the same way he learned the meaning of mercy; not that he whose mercy is from age to age was ignorant of mercy's meaning until then, but what he knew of its nature from all eternity, he learned by experience during his days on earth.

A reading from St Augustine's Commentary on the Gospel of St. John.
Tract 15, 10-12, 16-17 : CCL 36, 154-156.

A woman from Samaria came to draw water

A woman came to draw water. She is a type of the Church not yet justified, but already on the way towards justification. Now this is what the text is saying : she came in ignorance, she found him and he entered into conversation with her. Let us look at the meaning of this and see why a woman from Samaria came to draw water. The Samaritans did not belong to the Jewish race, for they were foreigners. It is part of the allegory that this woman, who stands for the Church, came from a foreign race, for the Church was to come from the Gentiles, and to the Jews its members were outsiders. Let us therefore hear ourselves spoken of in her; let us recognize ourselves in her, and let us in her give thanks to God for what we are. She was indeed an image, not the reality, for she was a foreshadowing of what was to come and this foreshadowing became truth. She believed in him, and he made her story into a parable for us. *She came to draw water*, quite simply to draw water, as men or women are accustomed to do.

Jesus said to her, Let me have a drink. His disciples had gone into the city to buy food. The Samaritan woman said to him : How is it that you, a Jew, should ask me for a drink, for I am a Samaritan? The Jews have no dealings with Samaritans. Let us consider the position of foreigners. The Jews would not even touch any of their utensils. And since the woman was carrying with her a vessel to draw water she was amazed, because here was a Jew asking her for a drink, which was not the custom of the Jews. Moreover, he who was asking her for a

227

drink was thirsting for her to believe. Finally, consider who it is who was asking for a drink. *Jesus replied and said to her : If you knew the gift of God, and who it is who says to you, let me have a drink, you would perhaps have asked him and he would have given you a drink of living water.*

He asks for a drink, and he offers a promise of a drink. He is in need of one, and he has himself so much to give that will more than quench her thirst. *If you knew the gift of God*, he says. The gift of God is the Holy Spirit. Up to now he has not been speaking openly to the woman. But gradually he penetrates into her heart. Perhaps now he is teaching her, for what could be kinder or more gentle than his words of exhortation : *If you knew the gift of God and who it is who says to you, let me have a drink, you might perhaps ask him to give you a drink and he might give you living water.*

From what source is he intending to give her to drink, if not from that of which it is said: *With you is the source of life?* For how shall they thirst who *drink their fill from the copious fountains of your dwelling?* He was promising her an unfailing supply, the fullness of the Holy Spirit, and she did not yet understand; and as she did not understand, how did she answer? *The woman said to him : Lord, give me that water, so that I may never be thirsty, nor have to come here to draw water any more.* Her poverty made her think of work, and her weakness made her reluctant to undertake it. If only she could hear the words : *Come to me, all you who labour and are overburdened, and I will refresh you !* Jesus was saying this so that she would not have to toil any longer; but she did not yet understand.

YEAR B. Jn 2 : 13-25

A reading from St Augustine's Commentary on the Psalms of
Ascent to the Temple.
Enarratio in Psalm. 130, 1-3; CCL 40, 1899-1900.

We are the living stones from which God's temple is built

My brothers, I have often warned you in my sermons on the
Psalms not to listen to the psalmist's voice as though he were an
individual singer, but to take it as the voice of all who belong
to the body of Christ. Since all are members of his body, he
speaks as a single person. He himself is both one and manifold,
for his members are many among themselves but one in him
who is unique. This is the mystery of God's temple; the apostle
says of it that *the temple of God is holy, and that temple you are*
— all of you, that is, who believe in Christ and whose faith
expresses itself in love. For believing in Christ means loving him.
The demons believed without loving and so, in spite of their
belief, they demanded: *What have you to do with us, Son of
God?* But ours must be a faith that leads to love. Not for us the
cry : *What have you to do with us?* Rather let us say : We belong
to you, you have redeemed us. All who have this kind of faith
are like the living stones that are built up into the temple of
God, or like the incorruptible wood used to construct the ark
no flood could submerge.

Men themselves are the temple where God's gifts are asked
for and received. The gift of eternal life is only granted to those
who pray in the temple of God; but the man who prays there is
the man who prays within the peace of the Church, in the unity
of the body of Christ which consists of the multitude of believers
throughout the whole world. Such a man gains a hearing, for he
prays in spirit and truth. To pray in the temple of Jerusalem
gave no such assurance, for that temple was the scene of a

symbolic action in which the Lord drove out men because they were bent on their own ends, frequenting the place for the purpose of buying and selling. However, if that temple was a figure of the true one which is the body of Christ, it is apparent that even here men can be found who have only their own interests at heart, not those of Jesus Christ. Therefore, the Lord made a scourge of cords with which to drive such traders out of the temple.

The voice of the psalmist, then, belongs to the temple which is the body of Christ, and it is here, not in that temple built by hands, that God's gifts are sought and received in spirit and truth. The old temple was only the place of foreshadowing; consequently it has now been demolished. Does this mean that our house of prayer has been destroyed? Certainly not. How could that fallen temple be the one that was called *a house of prayer for all nations?* For you know what our Lord Jesus Christ said: *It is written, My house shall be called a house of prayer for all peoples, and you have turned it into a robbers' den.* Now the men who wanted to make the house of God a den of robbers surely did not intend to destroy the temple. Those who live evil lives within the Catholic Church are like them; they do their best to make the house of God into a robbers' den, but they do not on that account destroy it. The time will come when they will be driven out with the scourge of their own sins.

But as for the temple of God which is the body of Christ and the assembly of the faithful, it chants this psalm of ascent with the voice of a single man. We have already heard him in psalm after psalm; let us listen to him again now. If we wish, his voice is ours; we can listen to its music and sing it in our hearts. But if we refuse, we shall be like the traders in the temple of old, pursuing our own selfish interests. We may indeed enter the church, but it will not be in order to seek what is pleasing to God.

A reading from the Apostolic Constitution *Poenitemini* of Pope Paul VI.
AAS t. 58 (1966) pp. 179-180.

Repent and believe the Good News

Christ, who from the beginning of his life taught by word and example, spent forty days and forty nights in prayer and fasting before he undertook his mission. He inaugurated his public ministry with the joyful message : *The Kingdom of God is at hand;* but he immediately added the command : *Repent and believe the Good News.* These words are, as it were, an epitome of the entire Christian life.

We are allowed to reach the kingdom promised by Christ only through *metanoia,* that is, through an inward conversion of the whole person, by which we begin to think, judge and order our lives in that holiness and love of God which has now been revealed and fully communicated to us in his Son. The call to repentance made by the Son of God gains insistence from the fact that he preached penance both by exhortation and example. Christ indeed is the supreme model of penitents, for though he committed no sin himself, he willingly atoned for the sins of others.

When a man encounters Christ, he is illumined by a new light, and recognizes the sanctity of God and the malice of sin. Through Christ's word the call to conversion and offer of forgiveness are made to him. These graces are fully attained in baptism, which forms a man into the likeness of the Lord's passion, death and resurrection, so that his whole life bears the imprint of the paschal mystery.

Whoever calls himself a Christian must therefore follow his Master by denying himself, carrying his cross and taking his share of the sufferings of Christ. In this way he will be shaped into the pattern of the Lord's death, and so be enabled to share his risen glory. No longer ought he to live for himself, but for God, who loved him and gave himself up for him; he should also live for his neighbour, completing in his flesh what is lacking in Christ's afflictions for the sake of his body, the Church. Furthermore, since the Church is so closely bound to Christ, the penance of each believer inevitably affects the whole community. For not only in the Church does he receive the initial gift of *metanoia* in baptism, but also in the Church the same gift is restored and confirmed by the sacrament of penance in those members who have fallen into sin. "Those who approach the sacrament of penance obtain God's merciful pardon for the offences they have committed against him. At the same time they are reconciled with the Church, whom they have wounded by their sins, and who strives to obtain their conversion by her love, example and prayer." Finally, it is in the Church that the token satisfaction imposed on each penitent who receives this sacrament becomes in a special manner part of the expiation offered by Christ in heaven, while according to the Church's general dispensation each of the faithful may unite to his sacramental penance whatever else he may do, suffer or endure.

Thus the task of carrying the Lord's death about with him always, in body and soul, enters into every moment and every aspect of the entire life of the baptized Christian.

MONDAY

A reading from St John Fisher's Treatise concerning the Fruitful Sayings of David in the Seven Penitential Psalms.
Psalm CCXXIX.

If one of us should sin, we have an advocate with the Father

It is required both by right and equity that recompense be made for any fault or injury done to any person before the offence can be entirely forgiven, and for that reason a certain solemn feast was instituted under the old Law by Moses, according to God's commandment, to be celebrated and kept every year. They named it the feast of Making Clean, and the Day of Mercy. At this solemn feast it was customary to offer up a certain general sacrifice for the sins of all the people. On that day, when the high priest of their Law had hallowed certain live beasts in an outer part of the temple, he presently, arrayed in solemn apparel, entered alone into that area of the temple called the Holy of Holies, taking with him some of the beast's blood, which he sprinkled seven times before the throne of God which they called the Place of Mercy, so that he might more easily move almighty God to show mercy on his people. That was why they named this solemn feast the Day of Mercy.

All this sacrifice offered by the high priest under the old Law was only a figure, and, as we read in the Epistle to the Hebrews, a sign or token of the known truth to come. Therefore, Christian people, since our time now is the plenteous time of grace, we cannot be in a worse condition than the Jews were. In their time Almighty God was appeased by means of their sacrifice. Much more now in our days, when grace is superabundant, will he purge away our sins, for we have a sacrifice of much more strength and virtue; also it will sooner move Almighty God to exercise his mercy towards us.

Let us remember who is our high priest, what is our sacrifice, what manner of blood it is, what is the inward part of the temple, and to what intent all these things were ordained. We find the answer in the marvellous epistle written to the Hebrews. Christ Jesus is our high priest, his most precious body is our sacrifice, which he offered upon a cross for the redemption of all the world. The blood shed for our redemption was not the blood of goats or calves, as under the old Law, but it was truly the most innocent blood of our Saviour Jesus Christ. The temple in which our high priest offered sacrifice was not made by man's hand, but by the power of God alone. He shed his precious blood for our redemption before the face of the whole world, which is the temple made only by the hand of God. This temple has two distinct parts: one is the earth which we inhabit; the other is not yet known to us mortal creatures. First, he offered sacrifice on the earth when he suffered his Passion. Afterwards, in a new clothing or garment — the vesture of immortality — and with his own precious blood, he entered into the Holy of Holies — that is to say, into heaven — where he presented seven times this most precious blood before the throne of his Father, the blood which he shed for all sinners. By this holy sacrifice Almighty God will assuredly be moved to have pity and show mercy on all true penitents; and this sacrifice shall ever continue, not only year by year as in Jewish times, but it is also offered daily for our comfort, and every hour for our most powerful succour. That is why St Paul says: *By it we are redeemed for ever.*

Every contrite and truly penitent person, who is anxious not to fall again into sin but is wholly determined to continue in a virtuous life, is a partaker of this holy sacrifice. As St John says in his first Epistle: *My dear children in God, I write to you, warning you to abstain from sin; and if at any time, by your own negligence, you sin against God, call upon Jesus Christ,*

234

our advocate in heaven with the Father, who offered himself in
sacrifice for our sins, and not only for ours but also for the sins
of all the world.

YEAR II

A reading from the Sermons of St Augustine.
Sermo 205, 1 : In quadragesima 1 : Edit. Maurist. t. 5, 919-920.

Our crucifixion must continue throughout our life, not for forty days only

Today, as we begin our solemn Lenten observance, it is my
pastoral duty to nourish your minds with the word of God. It is
all the more important for me to do this when you are going to
mortify your bodies with fasting, and it is necessary for you to
renew yourselves spiritually with wholesome food, so that you
may more effectually curb your natural inclinations. As we
approach the passion of our crucified Lord, it is in keeping with
our purpose that we crucify ourselves by repressing our bodily
desires. As the apostle says, *You cannot belong to Christ Jesus*
unless you crucify all your self-indulgent passions and desires.
    A Christian, beset as he is with so many temptations, should
hang on this cross from the beginning to the end of his life. Not
for him, as long as he lives, to be rid of those nails we read of in
the psalm : *Pierce my flesh with the nails of your fear.* Flesh
means our bodily desires; nails, what God's justice requires of
us. These are the nails which must pierce our flesh with the fear
of the Lord and nail us to the cross as an acceptable sacrifice to
him. This is what the apostle urges us to do: *I appeal to you,*
brothers, by the mercy of God, to offer your bodies as a living
sacrifice, holy and acceptable to God. This is the crucifixion of
which the servant of God speaks, one in which he glories, not

one which throws him into confusion. *Far be it from me*, he says, *to glory in anything except in the cross of our Lord Jesus Christ, through whom the world has been crucified to me, and I to the world.*

This crucifixion is something that must continue throughout our life, not for forty days only. The reason why Moses, Elijah and our Lord himself fasted for forty days is this: that we might learn from Moses, Elijah and Christ — that is, from the Law, the Prophets, and the Gospel itself — not to imitate the ways of the world. On the contrary, they teach us to go on crucifying the unregenerate man within us.

Christians must always live in this way, without any wish to be rid of their cross, otherwise they will sink beneath the world's mire. But if we have to do so all our lives, we must make an even greater effort during these days of Lent. It is not a simple matter of living through forty days: Lent is an epitome of our whole life.

TUESDAY

YEAR I

A reading from the Commentary of St Cyril of Alexandria on the Gospel of St John.
Lib. 11, cap. 8 : PG 74, 505-508.

Christ is himself both sacrifice and priest

Christ is the mediator between God and man, our truly great and most holy high priest. As man he intercedes for us, and offering himself in sacrifice for our sake, he appeases his Father's anger by his prayers. For he is himself both sacrifice and priest, both mediator and victim without blemish, the true lamb who takes away the sin of the world.

We see, therefore, that the mediation of Moses in ancient times was a clear type and symbol of the mediation of Christ as manifested in the last days, and that the high priest of the law was a figure of the high priest who is above the law. Indeed, all that relates to the law is a foreshadowing of the truth. For those great and holy men, Moses and Aaron, always stood between God and the people of Israel. They placated God's anger at the people's sins, calling on heaven to be merciful to their weakness; they invoked blessings on them and offered the sacrifices and gifts ordained by the law for sins, or as thank-offerings for the blessings God had given them.

But Christ, who appeared in the last days to supersede the types and symbols of the law is both high priest and mediator. As man he intercedes for us, but as God he is one with God the Father in bestowing blessings upon those who are worthy of them. Paul's saying, *Grace and peace be with you from God our Father and from the Lord Jesus Christ* teaches us this quite clearly. Christ prays for us as man, but as God he also gives. For being a high priest who is holy, innocent, and undefiled, he did not offer himself in sacrifice for his own frailty, as did those to whom it fell to offer sacrifice according to the law. No, it was for the salvation of our souls, and on account of our sin that he made this offering, and made it once for all. *He undertook to plead on our behalf, and he is himself the sacrifice for our sins, and not for our sins only, but also for the sins of the whole world*, for the sins of every nation and race that is called to attain righteousness and holiness through faith.

A reading from a Sermon of St Peter Chrysologus.
Sermo 43 : PL 52, 320, 322.

Prayer knocks at the door, fasting gains entrance,
compassion obtains its request

My brethren, there are three things that give us stability in faith, constancy in devotion, perseverance in virtue : these three are prayer, fasting and compassion. Prayer knocks at the door, fasting gains entrance, compassion obtains its request. Prayer, compassion and fasting, these three are one and give life to each other. For fasting is the soul of prayer, and compassion is at the heart of fasting. No one can separate them; they cannot be divided. He who attains only one of them and not all three has nothing. The man who prays, then, must fast; the man who fasts must show compassion; the man who hopes his petition will be heard must listen to him who asks; the man who gains audience of God is he who does not refuse access to any who seek him.

The man who fasts must understand what fasting is; he must feel pity for the hungry if he wants God to feel pity for his own hunger. If he hopes for mercy, let him be merciful; if he looks for tenderness, let him be tender. If he wishes to receive let him give; only an impudent beggar demands for himself what he refuses to another.

Let each one of you be his own pattern of compassion : consider how you would wish mercy to be shown to you, how much and how urgently, then yourself show the same mercy to others as speedily and as fully. So let prayer, compassion and fasting become a single plea for us before God, a single presentation of our case, a single but threefold petition. What we lost by our meanness let us recover by our fasts; let us make our very souls a sacrifice by fasting, for there is no more excellent offering we could make to God, as the prophet confirms when he says: *A sacrifice to God is a broken spirit; a contrite and humbled heart God does not despise.*

Let each one of you offer his soul to God together with fasting, to make his gift a pure oblation, a holy sacrifice, a living victim. When you have made such an offering, it will still remain in your keeping. There is no excuse for not doing so, since the man who is prepared to give himself cannot fail to possess himself. Yet so that prayer and fasting may be accepted, compassion must accompany them. Fasting is a seed that does not germinate unless it is watered by compassion. When compassion runs dry, fasting becomes arid, for what rain is to the soil compassion is to fasting. However much the man who fasts may tend his soul, cut back his passions, root out his vices, sow the seeds of virtue, if he has not watered the ground with compassion he will gather no fruit. You may be sure that the field of your soul also fasts if it is deprived of compassion when you fast; but what you have poured out by way of compassion when you fast comes back to you in a rich harvest. Therefore, each one of you, since whatever you hoard you can only lose, be the gainer by your very prodigality. Give to yourselves by giving to the poor, for anything you have not given away to another you will find you cannot keep for yourself.

WEDNESDAY

A reading from 'The Adoration and Worship of God in Spirit and in Truth' by St Cyril of Alexandria.
Lib. 3 : PG 68, 289-292

*Christ offered himself for us, submitting to death
of his own free will*

Glorious things are spoken of you, O city of God. The wonderful and sacred city of which the divine David sang is the Church, and its inhabitants are we who, having been sanctified by the living bread, are protected by God from the destroying angel. Now that the time has come for the revealing of the holy Eucharist he has no further power to conquer us, for within us dwells Christ, who is life and the giver of life.

Seeing that the human race was being destroyed by death, Christ became our advocate with the Father; he offered himself for us, submitting to death of his own free will, having made the Destroyer believe that he was himself guilty of man's sin. This does not mean that he had sinned, but rather, as the Scriptures say, that *he bore the weight of our sins and suffered on our behalf, and was taken for a criminal.* Innocent though he was, *for our sake he became accursed.* This explains David's saying that the shepherd should suffer rather than the sheep, for Christ, like a good shepherd, laid down his life for his sheep.

In obedience to God's command, the divine David set up an altar in the place where he had seen the angel of destruction standing idle, and he offered holocausts and peace-offerings to God. By this place, which was a threshing-floor, we must understand the Church, for it is there that death is halted and overcome, even as the Destroyer long ago stayed his terrible and

240

devastating hand. For the Church is the dwelling-place of Christ, the dwelling-place of him who by his very nature is life.

Figuratively speaking, we say that the Church is a threshing-floor because, like ears of corn reaped by holy harvesters, people are gathered there after being converted from their former worldly life by the preaching of the apostles and evangelists. Then, when all superfluity in both word and deed has been removed, which is, as it were, the separation of the wheat from the chaff, the harvest is transported to the heavenly Jerusalem for storage in the courts on high, in the granary, so to speak, of the Lord.

Do you not say, Christ asked his holy apostles, *In four months it will be harvest-time? But look, I tell you, look at the fields : they are already white and ready for harvesting. Already the reaper is receiving his wages, he is gathering in a harvest for eternal life.* On another occasion he said : *The harvest is plentiful, but the labourers are few. It is for you therefore to beg the Lord of the harvest to send men out to reap it.*

Now as I understand it, the harvest Christ spoke of is a spiritual one, namely, the great multitude of those who would one day believe in him. The holy reapers are those who have in their minds and on their tongues the word of God, which *is living and active, and cuts more keenly than any two edged sword, piercing to the meeting-place of soul and spirit, to the innermost recesses of a man's being.*

Christ purchased the spiritual threshing-floor, which is the Church, as David did his, for fifty shekels : in other words, he paid for it dearly. For he gave himself for the Church, he set up an altar within her, and since he was both the priest and the sacrifice, he offered himself as though he were the beast that treads out the corn on the threshing-floor, and he became a holocaust and a peace-offering.

A reading from the first book of St Theophilus of Antioch 'To Autolycus'.
Lib. 1, 2. 7 : Grant, 2, 4, 10.

Blessed are the pure of heart, for they shall see God

If you say to me, 'Show me your God', my answer is, 'Show me the kind of man you are, and then I will show you my God. Show me that the eyes of your soul can see, and that the ears of your heart can hear.'

Those whose bodily eyes have the power of sight observe things that happen during our life on earth. At a glance they can tell the difference between light and darkness, white and black, beauty and deformity, symmetry and the lack of it, excess and deficiency. Likewise by the sense of hearing they distinguish between sounds, noticing whether they are strident, raucous, or pleasant. And it is the same with the ears of the heart and the eyes of the soul, for they have it in their power to see God.

God can be seen by men when the eyes of their souls have been opened. Now all men have eyes, but because the eyes of some are veiled by cataracts, they cannot see the light of the sun. Nevertheless, the fact that the blind cannot see it does not mean that there is no sunlight. On the contrary, the blind can only blame the deficiency of their own eyes. And so it is with the eyes of your soul when they are veiled by your sins and misdeeds. Just as a mirror needs to be polished, so a man's soul needs to be kept clean. When there is dust on a mirror a man cannot see his face in it; neither, when there is sin on his soul, can a man see God.

But you can be cured of your blindness if you have the will. Put yourself into the hands of the physician and he will open the eyes of your soul and your heart. Do you wonder what physician can do this? God can do it, for, through his Word and his Wisdom, he gives healing and life. Through his Word and his Wisdom he created the universe, *for the heavens were made by his Word; their whole array was made by his Spirit.* His Wisdom is all-powerful; *God founded the earth by Wisdom, he set the heavens in their place by understanding. His knowledge made the primeval depths burst forth, and the clouds drop down dew.*

If you understand these things, and live a pure, holy and upright life, you will be able to see God. But faith and the fear of God must first find a place in your heart, and all this will then become clear to you. So, when the time comes for you to lay aside your mortal nature and put on immortality, you will see God in so far as you deserve to see him. For God will raise up your body and make it immortal together with your soul, and then, when you have become immortal, you will see the Immortal, provided that you believe in him now.

THURSDAY

YEAR I

A reading from the Paschal Homilies of St Cyril of Alexandria. Hom. 26, 3 : PG 77, 925.

Christ became a merciful high priest

For our sake Christ became a merciful high priest. The law given to the people of Israel through the mouths of angels ordered the immediate punishment of those who fell into sin. As Paul bears witness: *The man who violates the law of Moses is put to death on the evidence of two or three witnesses.* So it was that priests under the law never had the least thought of showing mercy to anyone convicted of negligence. But Christ became a merciful high priest.He did not punish men for their sins, but justified all by his grace and compassion. Moreover, he taught us how to worship in a spiritual way, and by giving us a clear vision of the truth, he showed us how to live worthily. This is the message of the gospel.

Nevertheless, by teaching us the truth he did not mean to censure the law of Moses, or to refute the ancient prophets. It was a question rather of removing the shadow that overlay the writings of the law, and of replacing symbols by worship in spirit and in truth. He made this perfectly plain when he said: *Do not imagine that I have come to abolish the law or the prophets. I have not come to abolish them, but to fulfil them. I assure you that the law will not lose a single dot or stroke until its purpose is achieved.* We see then that by changing types into the reality they signified he was not nullifying, but fulfilling them. A painter, by covering his basic design with a variety of colour, does not destroy it but brings it out more clearly, and this is what Christ did when he transformed the crudity of symbols into the reality they represented.

Yet the people of Israel failed to understand this mystery, even though it had been foretold in many ways by both the law and the prophets. Indeed Christ our Saviour himself tried to show them through many marvellous deeds that although for our sake he had become man, according to the divine dispensation, he was still God as he had always been. To help them to realize this he did things that were beyond the power of any man — God alone could perform such miracles. He raised dead men from their graves when they were already in a state of corruption; like the Creator, he made blind men see the light of day; he rebuked unclean spirits with authority; he cured lepers by a word of command; and there were other things he did that were marvellous beyond all telling. Therefore, *If I am not acting as my Father would*, he said to them, *do not believe in me. But if I am, even if you do not believe in me, accept the evidence of my deeds.*

YEAR II

A reading from Tertullian's Treatise on Prayer.
Chapter 28-29 : CCL 1, 273-274.

The spiritual oblation

Prayer is the spiritual oblation which has done away with the sacrifices of ancient times. *What is the profusion of your sacrifices to me? says the Lord. I have had a surfeit of burnt offerings of rams; I have no desire for the fat of lambs nor the blood of bulls and goats. Who has demanded these things from you?* The gospel tells us what God requires of us : *The hour is coming,* it says, *when true worshippers will worship the Father in spirit and in truth. For God is Spirit, and such,* therefore, *are the worshippers he seeks.*

We are the true worshippers and the true priests. We offer a sacrifice of prayer in the Spirit, a sacrifice worthy of God and acceptable to him, one that God himself has asked for and has, in fact, made possible. Such is the sacrifice we are obliged to bring to God's altar : an offering dedicated with our whole heart, nurtured by faith, prepared in truth; unblemished in its innocence, spotless in its chastity, garlanded with love, accompanied by psalms, hymns and a procession of good works. God will then give us all that we ask.

He will deny nothing to prayer made in spirit and truth, since this is what he asks of us. How many are the reports of its effectiveness we read and hear, and to which we give credit! Under the Old Covenant prayer brought deliverance, no doubt,

from disasters such as fire, famine or wild beasts, even though
it had not received its form from Christ. Far greater is the effect
of Christian prayer — not in sending an angel to bring cooling
dew in the midst of fire, nor in stopping the mouths of lions, nor
in transporting the dinner of harvesters to hungry prisoners, nor
by the grace it obtains in warding off the experience of suffering,
but in furnishing those who suffer and grieve and feel pain with
the capacity to endure. It increases the power of grace, making
us understand what faith can obtain from the Lord, and the
meaning of the sufferings we bear for the name of God.

In the past, prayer brought about plagues, routed enemy
armies and caused droughts. Now the prayer of a just man turns
aside the entire wrath of God, pleads at night for enemies, and
intercedes for persecutors. If once the power of prayer called
down fire from heaven, what wonder that it can wring water
from the skies? Prayer is the one weapon that can conquer God.
But it was Christ's will that it should work no harm; the power
with which he invested it was for all that is good. And so
its only skill is in the art of bringing the dead back to life,
straightening cripples, healing the sick, casting out unclean
spirits, opening prison doors, freeing innocent captives. Prayer
cleanses us from sin, parries temptation, quells persecution,
strengthens the faint-hearted, gives joy to generous souls, brings
home wayfarers, calms the ocean waves, overpowers robbers,
feeds the poor, guides the rich, raises the fallen, upholds the
wavering, preserves those who stand their ground.

Even the angels pray, all of them; the whole creation prays —
beasts wild and tame bend their knees and, as they come out of
their stables and dens, look up to heaven with open mouths,
uttering sounds after their own fashion. The awakening birds
are also borne heavenwards, making the sign of the cross with
their wings in lieu of hands and emitting calls which may seem
like prayer.

What more can be said of the duty of praying? Even the Lord himself prayed. To him be honour and power for ever and ever.

FRIDAY

A reading from the Homilies of St John Chrysostom on the Second Letter to the Corinthians.
Hom. 2, 4-5; PG 61 : 397-399.

The power of prayer

God is often won over by the importunity of a number of people praying together in unison of mind and voice. We should therefore be eager to meet for prayer and to pray for each other as the early Christians prayed for the apostles. In this way we shall fulfil the commandment, and be stimulated to love; and when I say love, I include under that heading everything that is good. We shall also learn to be more earnest in thanksgiving.

If men give thanks for the blessings given to others, they do so even more for what they themselves have received. This was the case with David, who said: *Come, magnify the Lord with me, and let us praise his name together.* It is what the apostle urges in all his letters, and it should be our practice also. Let us proclaim God's blessings to all, so that we may gain companions in praising him.

If whenever we experience anything good at the hands of men our praise fills them with renewed zeal, we may be sure that to declare God's benefits will increase his favours towards us all the more. And if when we have been well-treated by men we urge others to join us in thanking them, surely we should show even more enthusiasm in leading as many people as we can to give thanks to God on our behalf. St Paul enjoyed confident freedom of speech before God, yet this was his practice; how much more then should it be ours.

Let us therefore entreat the saints to give thanks on our behalf, and ourselves do the same for each other. This greatest of all good works is a task that belongs especially to the priesthood. When we approach God, we first give thanks for the whole world and the good things we share in common — for each of us receives God's gifts in common with others, even our own personal salvation. We should render thanks to God together with others, therefore, for our own particular blessings, and praise him in private for the blessings that are common to us all. The sun does not shine for one person alone, but for all together. Although only part of the sun is visible to each man, he sees it as a whole; indeed it was precisely for the common good that it was made so large. It appears the same size to one man by himself as it does to all. The consequence to be drawn is that each personally owes as great a debt of gratitude to God as all men collectively, and it is only fitting that we should also give thanks for the shared gifts and for the integrity of other people's lives.

Often the blessings we receive are due to others. If there had been only ten just men in Sodom, it would not have suffered the fate it did. So let us give thanks too for the freedom and confidence that others show towards God, for this is an ancient rule of conduct which the Church adopted from the beginning, and which St Paul put into practice when he prayed for the Romans, the Corinthians, and for the whole world.

A reading from the Commentary on the Gospel of St John by
St Cyril of Alexandria.
Lib. 11, 10 : PG 74, 544-545.

For our sins, Christ sanctified himself

For their sake, said Christ, *I sanctify myself*. In terms of the law,
any offering made to God was said to be sanctified. An obvious
example of this was the offering made by the people of Israel of
all their first-born children. *Sanctify all the first-born to me*, God
commanded his holy servant Moses. In other words, consecrate
and offer them, set them apart as sacred.

Therefore, since sanctification was regarded as the equivalent
of consecration and setting apart, we may say that in this sense
the Son of God sanctified himself for our sake; for he offered
himself as a victim, a holy sacrifice to God the Father, and by
so doing, he reconciled the world with the Father, and restored
the fallen race of man to his friendship. *For he*, Scripture says, *is
our peace*.

We must realize, however, that our return to God is not
accomplished by Christ our Saviour except through the Spirit
in which he causes us to share and by which we are sanctified,
for it is the Spirit that binds us to God, and, in a real way, makes
us one with him. By receiving the Spirit through the Son, we
become sharers in the divine nature and, in the Son, we receive
the Father also.

*We know that we are in him and he is in us because he allows
us to share his own Spirit*. So writes St John, who had such deep
insight into these things; and St Paul adds : *Because you are sons,
God has sent the Spirit of his Son into your hearts, the Spirit
that cries out, 'Abba, Father'*. If we had remained without a
share in the Spirit, we should have had no experience of God's

presence within us; nor could we ever have become the sons of God had we not been enriched by the Spirit to whom we owe that title. How indeed could we have been adopted as sons and enabled to share in the divine nature if God did not dwell within us, and if we had not been united to him by being called to receive a share in the Spirit?

Now, however, we have part in the Godhead, and are declared to be the temples of God. For the only-begotten Son sanctified himself on account of our sins; in other words, he consecrated and offered himself as a holy and fragrant sacrifice to God the Father. In this way he removed the barrier of sin that separated man from God, so that henceforward there was nothing to impede us from drawing near to him and adhering to him in close communion. We do this through our participation in the Holy Spirit, who transforms us into upright and holy men, and enables us to bear once more the divine image in which we were created.

For if sin separates man from God, righteousness will surely be a bond of union with him, and a means of setting us at his side with no division between us. We have been justified, Scripture declares, by our faith in Christ, who *was delivered up for our sins and raised for our justification.* In him, as the first-fruits of the human race, the whole of man's nature was restored to newness of life. It was as though it returned to its very beginnings and was re-created in order to be sanctified.

SATURDAY

A reading from St Augustine's Commentary on the Psalms.
Ps. 85, 1 : CCL 39, 1176-1177.

Jesus Christ prays for us, he prays in us,
he is prayed to by us

God could not possibly have done more for men than to offer them as their Head the Word by which he had created all things, and to make them the members governed by that Head. By this gift he who was Son of God would also become son of man, one with the Father in his divinity and at the same time one with mankind in their humanity. When we speak to God in prayer, therefore, we do not separate the Son from the Father. And when prayer is offered by the body of the Son, that body does not regard its Head as separated from itself. Our Lord Jesus Christ, the Son of God, is one in himself, the saviour of his own body. He prays for us and in us, even though we pray to him as well. He prays for us as our High Priest; as our Head he prays as part of us; and as our God we pray to him. Thus we should recognize our voices in his voice and his in ours.

And when, especially in the prophecies concerning him, we hear something said of the Lord Jesus Christ that attributes to him some quality of lowliness incompatible with God's majesty, we must not hesitate to understand it of one who, for his part, showed no hesitation in becoming one of us. He is able to use all created things to serve his ends, since all are of his making.

We are assured of his glorious divinity each time we hear the words: *In the beginning was the Word, and the Word was with God; the Word was God. He was with God from the beginning. All things were made by him, and without him was created nothing.* In words like these we are made aware of the divinity of the Son of God, of his sublimity and transcendence, of his immense superiority over all created things however marvellous; yet in other parts of Scripture the same Son is portrayed as sorrowing, praying and crying out in agony. And, it may be, we are tempted to avoid applying such passages to him, because our thoughts, raised up high by the contemplation of his divine majesty, are reluctant to come down to earth to consider the lowliness of his humanity. It seems almost an insult to apply such texts to him as man, before whom as God we have but recently lain prostrate in prayer. So for the most part we tend to turn our minds away and try to modify our standards of interpretation : no such scripture text must be applied to him if we can help it, unless it points directly to him and can by no means be deflected from him.

But let us rouse ourselves and open our eyes to the light of faith. Then we shall see clearly how he who not long before appeared as God has now assumed the semblance of a slave; he has taken to himself a human form and now behaves in every way as man; he has humbled himself, even going to the length of submitting himself to death. And while hanging on the cross he went still further and made his own the psalmist's words : *My God, my God, why have you abandoned me?*

As God, then, he receives our prayers, as simple man he offers prayers himself. On the one hand he is the Creator, on the other he has become a creature; without the need for any change or alteration in his divinity, he has adapted to himself our change-able creaturehood, and he has gathered us up into himself, to become with him one single man, head and body. Thus we pray to him, through him, and in him; our voice is heard along with his and his with ours.

A reading from a Sermon by St Gregory Nazianzen on the Love of the Poor.
Oratio 14, 38, 40 : PG 35, 908-909.

Let us serve Christ in the person of the poor

Blessed are the merciful, Scripture says, *for they shall receive mercy.* Mercy is not the last of the virtues to be counted among the beatitudes. Another text reads: *Blessed is he who cares for the poor;* and another: *The good man is moved by pity to be generous. He is ready to lend all day long.* Therefore let us lay hold of this blessing and be known for our understanding, kindness and compassion.

Even the night should not interrupt your works of mercy. Never say: *Come back again, I will give you something tomorrow.* Let us carry out our good intentions immediately. Kindness is the one thing that needs no second thoughts. *Share your bread with the poor and open your doors to the homeless,* and do it with good will. *If you give to charity,* says St Paul, *give cheerfully,* for willingness will double the effect of your good deeds. How insulting, how ungracious it would be to give reluctantly or under duress!

So then, let us go about our good works in a joyful spirit, not with a face of woe. If, in the words of Scripture, we *loose the bonds of those who stretch out their hands to us,* or as I interpret this text, if our charity is not mean and suspicious, full of doubts and grumblings, what then? Our reward will indeed be great and wonderful. *Then our light shall break forth like the dawn, and soon we shall grow healthy like a wound newly healed.* Light and healing: surely these are what we all long for?

If, then, my words can convince you, servants of Christ, brothers and joint-heirs of his, while we have the opportunity let us visit Christ, care for him, feed and clothe him, give him hospitality and cherish him. Not with a single meal as the Pharisees did, nor with perfumes like Mary, nor with a bare tomb like Joseph of Arimathea, nor with the burial spices of that half-disciple of Christ, Nicodemus. Nor indeed are we expected to produce the gold, incense and myrrh that the Wise Men brought to Bethlehem before any of these; but since the Lord of all requires mercy rather than sacrifice, and since pity is worth more than a holocaust of fat lambs, we can offer him our compassion by caring for the destitute and the outcasts of our society. So when we depart from this world they will receive us into the dwellings of eternity, in the person of Christ our Lord. To him be glory for ever! Amen.

LENT

TWO YEAR SCRIPTURE CYCLE
LENT : PART I

YEAR 1   YEAR 2

ASH WEDNESDAY
Is 58, 1-12

THURSDAY
Deut 1: 1, 6-18   Exod 1: 1-22

FRIDAY
Deut 4: 1-8, 32-40   Exod 2: 1-22

SATURDAY
Deut 5: 1-22   Exod 3: 1-20

FIRST WEEK OF LENT

Deut 6: 4-24	Sunday	Exod 5: 1-6: 1
Deut 7: 6-14; 8: 1-6	Monday	Exod 6: 2-13
Deut 9: 7-21, 25-29	Tuesday	Exod 6: 29-7: 25
Deut 10: 12-11:7, 26-28	Wednesday	Exod 10: 21-11: 10
Deut 12: 1-14	Thursday	Exod 12: 1-20
Deut 15: 1-18	Friday	Exod 12: 21-36
Deut 16: 1-17	Saturday	Exod 12: 37-49; 13: 11-16

SECOND WEEK OF LENT

Deut 18: 1-22	Sunday	Exod 13: 17-14: 9
Deut 24: 12-25: 4	Monday	Exod 14: 10-31
Deut 26: 1-19	Tuesday	Exod 16: 1-18, 35
Deut 29: 2-6, 10-29	Wednesday	Exod 17: 1-16
Deut 30: 1-20	Thursday	Exod 18: 13-27
Deut 31: 1-15, 23	Friday	Exod 19: 1-19; 20: 18-21
Deut 32: 48-52; 34: 1-12	Saturday	Exod 20: 1-17

THIRD WEEK OF LENT

Hebrews 1: 1-2: 4	Sunday	Exod 22: 20-23: 9
Heb 2: 5-18	Monday	Exod 24: 1-18
Heb 3: 1-19	Tuesday	Exod 32: 1-20
Heb 4: 1-13	Wednesday	Exod 33: 7-11, 18-23; 34: 5-9, 29-35
Heb 4: 14-5: 10	Thursday	Exod 34: 10-28
Heb 5: 11-6: 8	Friday	Exod 35: 30-36: 1; 37: 1-9
Heb 6: 9-20	Saturday	Exod 40: 14-36